COMMENTARY ON SINGAPORE

❸ Culture, Identity and Society

COMMENTARY ON SINGAPORE

❸ Culture, Identity and Society

Edited by

Gillian Koh

National University of Singapore Society, Singapore

NUSS The Graduate Club

World Scientific

Published by

World Scientific Publishing Co. Pte. Ltd.
5 Toh Tuck Link, Singapore 596224
USA office: 27 Warren Street, Suite 401-402, Hackensack, NJ 07601
UK office: 57 Shelton Street, Covent Garden, London WC2H 9HE

National Library Board, Singapore Cataloguing in Publication Data
Name(s): Koh, Gillian, editor.
Title: Commentary on Singapore / edited by Gillian Koh.
Description: Singapore : World Scientific Publishing Co. Pte. Ltd., [2024]
Identifier(s): ISBN 978-981-12-6454-2 (hardcover ; volume 1) |
ISBN 978-981-12-6559-4 (paperback ; volume 1) |
ISBN 978-981-12-6455-9 (ebook for institutions ; volume 1) |
ISBN 978-981-12-6456-6 (ebook for individuals ; volume 1) |
ISBN 978-981-12-8106-8 (hardcover ; volume 2) |
ISBN 978-981-12-8139-6 (paperback ; volume 2) |
ISBN 978-981-12-8107-5 (ebook for institutions ; volume 2) |
ISBN 978-981-12-8108-2 (ebook for individuals ; volume 2) |
ISBN 978-981-12-8703-9 (hardcover ; volume 3) |
ISBN 978-981-12-8732-9 (paperback ; volume 3) |
ISBN 978-981-12-8704-6 (ebook for institutions ; volume 3) |
ISBN 978-981-12-8705-3 (ebook for individuals ; volume 3)
Subject(s): LCSH: Singapore--History. | Singapore--Politics and government. |
Singapore--Foreign relations. | Singapore--Economic policy. | Environmental policy--Singapore. |
Singapore--Population. | Singapore--Social policy.
Classification: DDC 959.57--dc23

British Library Cataloguing-in-Publication Data
A catalogue record for this book is available from the British Library.

For any available supplementary material, please visit
https://www.worldscientific.com/worldscibooks/10.1142/13698#t=suppl

Desk Editor: Jiang Yulin

Typeset by Stallion Press
Email: enquiries@stallionpress.com

Printed in Singapore

Mission Statement

"To foster a lifelong relationship with NUS and the wider graduate community."

At NUSS, a lifelong relationship with NUS and the wider graduate community is achieved through two mutually reinforcing thrusts:

- Promoting the interests of its members and NUS; and
- Contributing positively to Singapore's political and intellectual development and helping to cultivate a more gracious social and cultural environment.

As the foremost graduate society, NUSS strives to promote the interests of its stakeholders by providing appropriate platforms for all to socialise, build networks, improve connectivity and exchange ideas through a multitude of recreational, academic, political, social and cultural activities.

Contents

Introduction

What you have in your hand is the third of a three-volume set of essays we hope will inform thought and debate on Singapore's future.

The essays were first published over several years in the National University of Singapore Society's (NUSS) journal called *Commentary* which has drawn on thought-leadership on topics to do with Singapore's political, economic, social, and cultural development as well as foreign relations.

The journal has several objectives that are an extension of those of NUSS itself — to promote the continued intellectual growth of its members as well as foster a gracious social and cultural environment.

NUSS and the Commentary team felt that in this age of rapid change not only in Singapore but the world, there were many essays in past editions of the journal that can provide intellectual ballast and also provoke fresh discussion on public policy among the broader Singaporean public as they have done for its membership even today.

The first volume was curated to provide historical context and analyses of Singapore's foreign policy, and in relation to that, views on the orientation, values, and interests that the new, fourth generation of national leaders may need as they address the challenges in this policy domain so critical to the city-state's survival. This, as the multilateral, liberal geopolitical global order that served the interests of a small and open economy, and cosmopolitan nation like ours, can no longer be taken for granted just as the traditional paradigms of work centred on more predictable structures of industrial and manufacturing activities have given way to adaptive, smart, and digital technologies of the Fourth Industrial Revolution also. We looked at how the political leadership might have to respond to the disruptions in policy orthodoxies and the political pressures that emerge from these trends.

The second volume takes readers on a tour of the specific strategies of economic development that were adopted to lift Singapore out of the dire conditions of a no-longer viable strategy of import substitution, to an export-driven manufacturing one after it separated from Malaysia in 1965. Plan B had to work but as the chapters also recount, there was a measure of environmental consciousness in translating those strategies into tangible improvements in the livelihoods of citizens. Re-publishing this set of essays in 2024 as the globe feels the extreme weather effects of climate change, one is grateful that policy measures to avoid the pollutive effects of early industrialisation and the vision of becoming a Garden City to symbolise Singapore's ability to exercise discipline and "cultivate" industry, workers and people towards productive outcomes have been in place for decades. Of course, given the trade-offs from being a global node in the bunkering business with its contribution to carbon emissions on behalf of its customers, and urban renewal and redevelopment for industry and homes with its cost to nature conservation, Singapore cannot argue that it has a clean sheet in relation to climate change. It can however argue that it has been conscious of those choices and has a framework that recognises that the environment matters. The essays in Volume Two set out how those policy dilemmas and others related to population and human resource development have been and must continue to be tackled wisely and at the same time. This, as the country ages and does not have the quality of talent at the scale it needs to achieve the ambitions of its people to have prosperous, progressive, and also ecologically sustainable lives.

Volume Three focuses on the all-important question: Why do any of this? The essays provide the wide-range of ways that thought-leaders in Singapore have tried to define "the nation", its sense of identity and collective purpose. The authors have proffered their responses, be it through the arts, analyses of our political narratives, discussions on economic strategy, visions of urban development, and acknowledgement of the contributions of civil society. Each tries to help us feel our way around what "Singapore" means; each tries to craft a sense of what has been, is, and ought to be.

The chapters go beyond the juridical or realist definition of the "sovereign state" of Singapore, which was the stuff of Volume One, or the materialist reality of being a competitive economy and a place that must provide a livelihood for its people which was the stuff of Volume Two. The authors of this volume help us transcend the divide between the governing and governed to discuss what constitutes the soul of the nation that must pull everyone together.

The late pioneer Deputy Prime Minister, S Rajaratnam said in 1967 that the key challenge confronting Singapore was the task of "converting a society of transient immigrants into a community of citizens"; that being a citizen of Singapore is "not a matter of ancestry but choice and conviction". What then are we to be convicted about? How is this sense of conviction created? Is it something that is fixed, built upon, and reinforced by other unyielding truths, or has it got to be re-defined or re-interpreted or re-possessed with each generation? Like the six blind men who defined the elephant only by the parts they felt, does the nature of this conviction depend on what one has experienced or are there some unifying, unchanging commonalities we share and rally around despite our diversity?

Terence Chong frames our volume in Chapter 1 by introducing us to The Artist since we have already heard from the politicians, historians, economists, and ecologists in the previous volumes. He highlights the struggle between the state and the Artist over defining our nation since the moment of Independence. He notes that the early political leaders mobilised the arts to create a society that would be "civilised" and "cultured". They sponsored these as nation-building projects, presenting artistic works around idealised notions of culture, often anchored in ethnicity. The arts allowed the Government to play out its multiracial fantasies, he says, which it thought was central to the Singapore identity. Chong highlights also the leaders' beliefs about state patronage — the common dictum that he who pays the piper calls the tune. They expected artists to create works accordingly. This functional orientation to the arts and culture persisted through to the 2000s and even in the landmark Renaissance City project not by dictating its content but arguing how it would anchor talented Singaporeans to the country as creators or consumers of the arts and attract innovators here to energise the development of the creative industries, the arts and more.

Art is also viewed as extensions of the artists' biography, and often with suspicion by the state. In that regard, Chong reminds us that the enduring ingredients of the Artist are "Truth and Suffering", of suffering for his or her art especially when it is his or her expression of the truth about society; in pricking the conscience of society; in resisting what is perceived to be the over-bearing force of society; in highlighting where society or state may have gone wrong or is being confronted by its own contradictions. Chong cites several examples of artists and their art which were written off as deviant or created by deviants in Singapore's history. Artists are not just about their gifts and talents but ultimately the right they claim to challenge dominant ideology and orthodoxies, he notes. Indeed, it makes them uncomfortable to live with, inconvenient to sponsor, but how will we know if the truth is really what we think it is or is portrayed to be by the state? For whom is anything the truth? How will we know especially if it is about values, culture, sensibilities, norms, and lived realities? Artists provide us with alternative narratives, visions, scenarios, presented on stage, in artefacts and texts that allow us to test what the truth is about ourselves, about our country and nation.

In Chapter 2, C. J. Wee Wan-Ling provides a more detailed but just as critical account of Singapore's arts and culture policies from the 1980s. While an organic, experimental arts scene was just emerging, new policies were introduced by the Government to foster artistic creativity and create an arts market, thinking that these would, in turn, encourage technological and entrepreneurial innovation. Within this lies what Wee calls, "the central tension between the professed wish for a dynamic creativity and an instrumental-rational mental set". Aesthetic values seemed displaced by the commercial values of the marketplace; autonomy and creativity so vital for profound artistic heights to be reached were stymied in Wee's opinion by what he terms "disciplinary, economics-oriented instrumental-rationality".

The concepts of "Primary" and "Original" are integral to art but they have little opportunity to flourish ironically because of the state's strategy of making Singapore, "a cultural hub". What does it matter if "national culture and the arts" become only commodities in the process of creating a suitable brand that attracts tourists, investors and immigrants; if it is just an extension of the strategy to transform itself, as Wee puts it, from a "colonial city into a modern if uni-functional premier 'world city'...an economic centre for business in the Asia-Pacific"? It matters. In an age of globalisation, the arts, the artists and their willingness to contribute something of their authentic selves to society are what will enable "the nation" to mark itself out, protect itself, and maybe even, thrive. The other option may be to simply turn Singapore into an "empty hub for other people's high or popular/mass culture to pass through". This, Wee argues, does not serve the government's goal of making Singapore a "world-class home" for Singaporeans to want to stay in. Authenticity is what resonates and is needed.

In spite of this, in Chapter 3, Alvin Tan believes there have been ways in which the Singapore Artist has been able to create his art, to create concepts of the nation, invent genre that speaks to what Singapore is. He shares how his theatre company, The Necessary Stage has contributed to the creation of intercultural theatre, as distinct from the multicultural theatre the Government has envisioned, and Chong and Wee have critiqued. Tan explains that whilst multiculturalism is the acknowledgement of different cultures existing in one geographical space, interculturalism refers to the interaction of different cultures, the latter being a more sophisticated concept that helps to "politically re-imagine how we can work and live across differences". He adds, "[t]his is an important instrument for us Singaporeans as we are not Japan, China, India, Hong Kong or Indonesia. We are not anchored in one mother culture as we have different cultures co-existing here". Therefore, "[o]ur national identity is seen as pretty fluid, open to being constructed through marriage and so, interculturalism would be best suited for a country/nation that is a product of the global village era." This provides us with the conceptual framework as well as the process by which we can explore again what it means to be a society of Chinese, Malays, Indians and "Others" as well as whatever unique hybridities have already emerged from these; what we are, and what we might wish to be and become. The most critical ingredient to this quest is that sense of agency, autonomy, and creation, from the ground up.

In Chapter 4, historian Kwa Chong Guan recounts how independent and modern Singapore was created not only in the practical sense of life after its Separation from Malaysia but in the world of ideas and national narrative led by the governing party's chief ideas man — the creative, visionary Mr S Rajaratnam. After prevailing over the most acute crises emanating from battles against colonialism, communism and communalism, Kwa provides an account of how the "PAP leaders acted to exorcise the ghost of Separation by disproving the deeply held historical assumption that Singapore, divorced from its peninsula hinterland, would collapse and prove instead that Singapore as a city-state could survive the odds."

By 1972, Rajaratnam crafted an elegant and compelling image of Singapore as a "new kind of city — the Global City", which as Kwa says, led to a "new ordering" of work, social and family lives that reconfigured the "social memories we inherited". The physical landscape as well as collective histories were replaced.

Kwa argues how this act of creation was so successful that subsequent leaders lived to regret it as younger generations of Singaporeans had little to remember how development and affluence had come about. After all, they need a grasp of the starting point to notice this as progress in relief. Without it, citizens may not have the wherewithal to replicate that energy to do the same in their lifetimes and nor can the political leadership benefit from the recognition of its contributions if it needed to.

Kwa sets out for us the rediscovery of Singapore's history by the Establishment which had two implications — it generated the drive among the vanquished in its political story to assert their place in it, and promote alternative reconstructions of that history; it also opened up room for all sorts of social actors including the artists, dramatists, poets, and film-makers to offer their interpretations and narratives of what Singapore is. If the Establishment wanted to put out its clear, definitive history and narrative of the past, contestation of it would be the necessary price to pay. Of course, this is to be welcomed in principle, and for those who have the luxury of time and intellectual capacity to engage in this, it is only fair to hear the other side(s). Others with less patience for such exercises in creating "the nation" may wonder why it is that the more that we go on, the less it is that we understand.

For the late journalist, Yang Razali Kassim however, whose essays are featured in Chapter 5 and Chapter 9, there are some things that are immutable and should be "created away". In the former which is an essay about envisioning Singapore in the year 2030, Yang states that language and culture are at the heart of the key values of multiracialism, multiculturalism and meritocracy. Fundamentally, Singapore's geographical and cultural location in the Malay world of Southeast Asia is a given, whatever narratives one seeks to come up with for the Singapore nation, and Yang deeply appreciates the fact that even within their acts of creation, the political leaders always recognised the foundational role of the Malay language — symbolised by how Singapore's prime ministers always began their national day rallies by speaking in the national language. This is in addition to the fact that the national anthem and even drills in the armed forces are expressed in Malay. He argues that it speaks of the tolerance and mutual accommodation that also signals how the other constituent cultures and peoples of Singapore are welcomed. This is a paradox that only insiders, that is, Singaporeans of the mind, heart and soul, can grasp. Yang hopes this will long be the case even in the face of changing demographics and immigration that have become part of the solution to Singapore's progress towards 2030.

In Chapter 9, Yang similarly argues that the issues of "national identity, multiracialism and national language" must remain central to the creation of what is a future Singapore when he wrote in the year the country marked its golden jubilee, 2015. He shares the personal side of his experience of living in rich and accommodative multiracialism, in school, in National Service, and at work. He noted that many had a grasp of simple, conversational Malay that helped everyone feel connected. He admits that over time, while Malay remains the national language, English has bridged ethnic and cultural divides and conversational Malay has receded in use. Singlish as well as Mandarin have come into greater use too. Yet, he notes that he has met Chinese who cherish the national language and was surprised to learn that a colleague from the Chinese language paper was taking up lessons in it.

Was he to be optimistic about the social integration of Singapore if he were to place store on this anecdote, he asks? He recognised that the rise of China and the nature of immigration trends in the country were such that Mandarin was of growing import. Yang cites former veteran diplomat Kishore Mahbubani arguing that it would be "abnormal" for the citizens of a country who say Malay is its national language to have no facility in it, and provides suggestions to promote wider public grasp of it — through annual campaigns, by encouraging Malays themselves to commit to improving the grasp of their own language as they grow in their use of English, recognising with pride that the Malay language was and will continue to be the regional lingua franca. Creation can arise from the rediscovery of one's roots.

Chapter 6 by Tay Kheng Soon does the opposite. In an essay from 2013, he spells out what he thinks are the emerging maladies of Singapore present and envisages a more ideal state of the country to suggest a way to overcome them. Those gaps in progress that the populace will face, he argues, are not just a widening income gap and even a knowledge gap. There is also a gap between the potential to be creative as the full expression of being human, and what seems to be a staid and even stifling environment where people seem "feckless" in this Singapore of the future.

In what Tay says is a work of fiction, he envisages Year 2022 (which of course is now past) when younger members of the administrative elite rediscover Singapore's history and culture to develop a new sense of consciousness and purpose. They adopt new planning models, eschewing the old ones that were appropriate for larger countries, to take advantage not only of smallness and density but more critically, of "synergy". This is achieved by stacking different activities together so that they resemble not a factory but a living organism — smart, complex, and linked-up as incubators of creativity. The effect, he imagines, is "electrifying", with new life bursting forth. It is expressive and entrepreneurial. The neighbourhoods are smart webs akin to the human nervous system: "retail commerce, social clubs, civic activities, educational provisions, humanitarian institutions and galleries all combine to produce a wonderful experience, everyday, for everyone". The cooperative movement associated primarily with the national trade union is scaled-up to provide jobs for life and skills development. These foster a new, happy and productive workforce in Tay's vision. Where the old value system of the 5Cs that moved Singaporeans in the early years of development was about the acquisition of materialist items viz. cash, credit card, country club, condominium and car, this was replaced by the attitudes of courage, curiosity, creativity, compassion and collaboration. Reforms in education, the civil service, and systems that support the ageing population follow. A new urban conurbation emerges in the Southern Waterfront of the island, housing a million people living in enhanced levels of synergy. Now, the survival of Singapore would be secured through a reliance on the country's "total intelligence" as it is properly networked across what were previously structured and zoned as disparate sectors and activities. Singapore becomes the crucible for creativity, enterprise, and human development; an innovation hub that even serves the region.

In 2024, has Tay's vision come to pass? We certainly see the emergence of the models that stack, weave, cluster and mix to enhance liveability and synergy in the design of community hubs like Our Tampines Hub and Kampung Admiralty. There is the promise of more to come like the multi-modal integrated transport corridors. These corridors are people-centred as seen in the North-South corridor that is currently under construction. Instead of being only an expressway for cars, there will now be walking paths for pedestrians, dedicated cycling trunk routes that take riders all the way into the city, and lanes solely reserved for public buses which will allow them to complete their journeys faster. With vehicular traffic diverted to a viaduct and tunnel, more communal and park spaces are going to be available at ground-level.

Digital neural networks that link industry, academia, the creatives, and possibly finance that Tay envisaged have yet to develop however, but they can only do so when the actors find each other to make common cause or are adventurous enough to create synergies by working together.

This is still a fascinating chapter to read because there is clearly a lot more work that is needed to generate the sort of synergy, power and excitement it speaks of. It is an attempt to create a new "Global City" moment which we think readers will find attractive.

Stirring, compelling narratives have the power to create nations and in Singapore, the same leader had to do it twice. In Chapter 7, Viswa Sadasivan reminds us that the merger narrative of founding Prime Minister Lee Kuan Yew and his lieutenants was at first, successful, but in no more than two years, "went up in smoke". Sadasivan writes: "This must certainly constitute a rare occurrence in political history when a narrative that was imbibed by the people had to be dismantled and promptly replaced by another narrative promulgated by the same leader! This is usually the recipe for the ignominious demise of a political leader. It was clearly not so in the case of Mr Lee and the PAP government."

It was the indomitable will of the people inspired by their leaders that explains Singapore's success subsequently, says Viswa. The challenge however is that the success has in turn meant that a fresh new narrative is needed now (and one that Tay and other authors in this volume offer). This need is indicated by the erosion of political support for the PAP, from the mid-1990s to the watershed 2011 election when the governing party lost seven seats to the opposition. It can only come about, he says, if the Government recognises how ground sensibilities have shifted; if it can tell the difference between the symptoms of the challenges from their causes; and if it has the interest and will to effect the change. It is no mean feat to craft yet another narrative that effectively resonates with the people and rekindles the bond between them and their leaders. He says it can only happen if it provides a clear sense of empathy with the people and is in sync with the ethical considerations of the day. More pointedly, he reminds us that people rally behind "ideas and ideals; more than products and services". Vision versus performance measures — which will the leaders of today appeal to? Do they have the political capacity to craft a compelling story not only of Singapore's past as Kwa says they seek to, but also its future amid change and a real sense that the old assumptions about delivering progress no longer hold?

This brings us to Chapter 8 by former veteran diplomat and one of the leading thinkers of the world, Kishore Mahbubani who kicks-off with what he says are two bold and controversial claims. First, it is that no other country has developed as rapidly and comprehensively as Singapore over the past five decades; and second, that if it continues on "autopilot", and "repeats the same goals and policies" as the past, it is "heading towards disaster". This is because the world has changed, he says.

Singapore was ahead of the curve when it began its development journey but now it needs "new sets of aspirations", he argues. People cannot continue to chase after the old 5Cs of the "Singapore Dream", and in this chapter, he illustrates the challenge using the specific dream of car ownership and therefore, the issue of Singapore's land transport policy as well as public attitudes to the solutions.

His view is that the Government had been too ideological in its approach — in believing that market solutions would solve this unquenchable thirst for a car in tiny Singapore, and provide the practical solutions in public transport. Public transport was privatised but the profit motive did not serve the situation well given the maintenance troubles that the Mass Rapid Transit system faced at the time of writing. Raising the cost of car ownership to manage demand only made having a car more desirous; a status symbol of having arrived in life. The solution: Find ways to curb the worship of cars, make the public transport system more intelligent and integrated, and have it attuned to even micro-level, local demand. The large revenues generated from taxing car ownership should be shunted to making public transport far more affordable. Finally, the Government should eschew the notion that the private sector can do a better job of delivering public transport, and in that vein, other public goods too.

The opportunity, he says, is that as Singaporeans' basic needs are met, they will be less consumed by accumulating more material goods anyway and more consumed by achieving the higher order needs of love, belonging, self-esteem and happiness — ideas and ideals. Are we certain that these shifts are possible within the Government and even desirous among the public?

This point provides further context for the essays in the volume — the Vision Thing, the meaning, the stories about what Singapore is and wants to be, gain greater prominence even as the question of achieving high standards of material well-being for its people is taken for granted. The demands on leaders have not actually shifted but have been added to. Living through the COVID-19 pandemic from 2020 to 2022, but also the severe disruptions to the supply of basic goods and energy from the Russia–Ukraine War that began in February 2022, and growing disillusionment with multilateralism and free trade around the world, the task before Singapore leaders across the sectors is not just the uni-dimensional task of achieving economic competitiveness and growth. It is an omni-dimensional task of delivering "happiness, prosperity and progress", that no government edict, corporate policy, or even the welfare state can address adequately. Dignity, autonomy, and self-fulfilment require far more than what the market or the state can deliver on their own or even together.

Having said that, in Chapter 10, we are reminded again that "the market" cannot be taken for granted either. While former Danish Ambassador to Singapore Joergen Oerstroem Moeller contributed this chapter in 2015, it still raises relevant issues related to economic competitiveness that must be dealt with to ensure that the material base for Singaporeans' aspirations is indeed secure. He highlights that it was good governance, an accurate reading of not just geopolitical trends but Singapore's comparative advantage rather than the presence or absence of the natural endowments of resources and factors of production that made the difference in Singapore's development story. In fact, Singapore turned its size and lack of resources on its head by very successfully adopting the concept of being a global hub as its strategy. We recall the late Mr Rajaratnam's vision of Singapore as a global city but also the late Albert Winsemius' Plan B of its export-oriented industrialisation strategy that powered that story — from being a manufacturing hub, it became a services hub, finance hub and then greater specificity was placed on becoming a health and education hub, Moeller notes. Each time, Singapore tried to capture first-mover advantage in the region, shifting adroitly into where opportunities presented themselves.

Even then, Moeller saw that these activities would be disrupted by a massive restructuring of global trade — from shorter value-chains, to greater focus on regional integration and near-shoring to manage strategic and geopolitical risks especially in the area of energy. The question for Singapore he felt was whether it would have some of the East Asian pie or would need to develop the Southeast Asian pie so that it creates new vectors of value and economic growth.

As we know in 2024, all of it matters as Singapore seeks to insert herself into emerging value-chains at all levels and layers of activities. She does not have the luxury of taking a bet on one and not the other. Perhaps more perceptively, Moeller discusses Singapore as the premier urban hub, a demonstration case for liveability, sustainability, and all things to do with human security. In the age of climate change, resource constraints, and societal fissures arising from identity politics and income insecurity, the chapter looks at what Singapore itself has to offer — not as a transit point but as a staging point for generating the solutions to complexities of human existence itself. This provides even greater impetus to achieving what Tay set out in Chapter 6.

Where will the leadership that must drive this change come from? The elite, the select, the rich, the "powerful"? Are citizens too ordinary to matter or do they have assets that have yet to be activated and mobilised for this new Singapore that the authors in this volume wish for? Are they where leadership is renewed or emerges from? The next section of the book focuses on the role of citizens — taking it upon themselves to build a better country and life.

In Chapter 11, Ho Kong Chong, Hasliza Ahmad, Helen Sim and Ho Zhi Wei remind us of who makes up the population on this island. With constant flows of immigrants into Singapore, some as temporary sojourners and others who choose to sink roots here, it is increasingly diverse in ethnicity and culture. This makes the need to foster social cohesion more difficult but more critical. Trust in society can quite easily be eroded especially if the cross-cultural interaction is kept minimal and is confined to single contexts. How can we counteract? The authors note that social participation and volunteerism do help to foster diverse friendships, a multicultural orientation, other interpersonal and leadership skills and integration into society. These cannot be taught in a classroom. They are caught in these other activities with diverse sets of peers. The strong social compact across society, the authors argue, will help Singapore's youth surmount the challenges of being a global city by achieving cohesion amid diversity. These ideas also link back to Tan's essay on interculturalism. Repeated interaction across diverse diversity can fragment, or it can lead to new forms of hybridity if we allow it, if we do not insist only on the compartments or categories that we began with.

Melissa Kwee asks in Chapter 12 the important "why" question — why do we do this? Five trends help people arrive at an answer to that question. First, the emergence of skills-based volunteerism where professionals use their expertise in social activism activates an organic process of merging the "good" we want to achieve across the corporate and people sectors. This coherence begins at the personal level. Second, the rise of youth volunteerism that adopts the service-learning methodology so that it is not about "robotically implementing programmes" but that there is an intentional process of reflection and meaning-making. Third, businesses are partnering each other to create a "city of good" in Singapore which means that competitive instincts can be set aside for a compelling social and moral vision. Fourth, families are rallying their members to do good and this is where the building of culture begins — in the home. Fifth, informal and community-based giving where volunteers are engaged directly with the ground and take up opportunities to make a difference with greater flexibility, detail, and direct connection with the beneficiaries is happening. These are antidotes to the "slacktivism" of just tapping the "like" button on the all-pervasive social media-based campaigns, or the complaining that we often hear as part of the national discourse on governance. Like those involved in the actions cited above, Kwee says it is worthwhile that those seeking to do good to pause, conduct some ground-level enquiry and understand the issues at hand before acting. As they go forward, she encourages citizens to discover the gifts that they already have within them or are in their possession to offer. This makes the endeavour of turning Singapore "a city of good" a relatable and achievable one; each citizen, an everyday hero to her neighbours, workmates, members of her corporate partners, with coherence in that spirit of giving.

This process of self-discovery of personal assets as well as the community's assets may seem counter-intuitive to many who may feel that the structures of society in Singapore are rigid — what your educational background is, determines your station in life, determines who your community becomes, sets up what you have materially and that is what matters. This volume of essays unearths how Singapore is now but also argues that it has to be so much more: values, vision, ideals and a belief that all are endowed with are far more than what can be captured by school certificates, business cards, what is in bank accounts.

Chapter 13 by Gerard Ee of the social service agency, Beyond Social Services, provides the greatest challenge to those social and political orthodoxies. Harking back to the old days in Singapore where people progressed by riding on social capital — the young found paid apprenticeships in workshops through word of mouth and went on to build careers and lives that way, Ee's approach to his work among disadvantaged communities is precisely to help them uncover this wealth that they actually possess. His plea is for us to "re-imagine the role of the social sector as one that increases the social capital within our country rather than one that simply services those on the margins...enable people from different segments and social strata to develop mutual trust and co-create solutions where they have an active role in their success." In the public rental housing estates where his work is based, he provides a platform for people to trust themselves and each other enough to pool their strengths, gifts and talents to do better together than if they just acted individually. This fosters "kindness, generosity, cooperation and forgiveness," says Ee, even as real-world problems are addressed. He provides the tangible illustration of how in a programme he runs, children in the community pour out all the savings once a month, pool that together and then divide it equally among all of them. The amount is tripled by a donor and then each of the members parks the sum into his or her Child Development Account which is then also matched by the Government. The children and broader community come to realise that what they have is now six times as much with all progressing together.

Ee offers four suggestions to the new generation of political leaders even as they have declared how much they want to uplift the needy. First, he urges them to safeguard community resources and infrastructure designed to achieve this than allow them to be used for other purposes. Second, safeguard the notion of community as a collective that has the power and decision-making capacity to deliver solutions for itself. Leadership facilitates this; it does not dictate it. Third, allow for transparency in identifying the problems that the community has to take hold of and resolve. This is instead of saying that experts will find solutions for them or that the leaders already have the solutions. Sharing openly and honestly is the first step to people being able to take hold of the issues and work out how they can address them. Finally, success only counts when all can reach the "finish line". Success is defined by the community that worked together to achieve it. Rather than a focus on the leaders and experts, in Ee's radical view, success in social work and arguably, societal development, is recognised by the compassion, social justice and all the people who have taken it upon themselves to make it happen.

In the same vein, yet from the point of view of the private philanthropist, Lee Poh Wah too suggests in Chapter 14 that there is a lot of autonomy and liberty to find fresh approaches to social needs when they are not bound so heavily by the burdens of public accountability, ideology, and path dependencies of how bureaucracies have "always done things". Independently-funded grantmakers have the means but also the fresh eyes to find innovative solutions even to old problems. Lee states, "as independent funders of diverse public goods, they provide alternative options to the solutions offered by the State, enlivening democracy and tempering government orthodoxy. Also, they possess the unfettered ability to engage in high-risk endeavours that impatient investors and fickle electorates shy away from."

Some of those social issues remain with us precisely because the old means and actors are at it, reluctant to let go of old paradigms, incredulously holding out for different outcomes in spite of that. Lee cites the work of the novel and expensive Circle of Care's interdisciplinary preschool system that the Lien Foundation has supported. Targeting, in the first instance, support for children from disadvantaged backgrounds, it melds the work of social workers, teachers, and therapists, focusing on their young charges but also the parents who in reality are an integral part of the equation of getting the kids to school and allowing them to achieve their developmental targets. The Foundation also funded the Kindle Garden which is an inclusive preschool that integrates children with special needs fully into its programmes. These efforts are driven by the common notion that early intervention works. For Lee, real philanthropy seeks to "liberate the receiver" and not "redeem the giver" through innovative, "mutant", intuitive grant-making which helps the social community unlearn the learning, reject mediocrity and complacency, and even becomes a spur for the Government to do better.

In Chapter 15, we have an account of the sort of informal, community-based, organic yet innovative community activism that Kwee and Ee refer to, and the spirit that undergirds what Lee appeals to in progressive philanthropy. Here, young citizens, namely, the Cassia Resettlement Team (CRT) have taken it upon themselves to help seniors who were relocated to new rental flats in Cassia Crescent because of the redevelopment of the public housing estate, that is the old Dakota Crescent, to rebuild a sense of community and provide social support. The authors, Lim Jingzhou and Rocky Howe explain how CRT bridges the gap between individual residents and what the formal social service agencies (SSAs) can provide but in ways that consciously avoid breeding a sense of dependency among the residents.

At the time of writing, they created circles of care of several volunteers to each vulnerable senior to help them cope with the sense of dislocation through practical support. They also convey the needs of the seniors to the SSAs that are providing formal care. CRT also ran a programme to discuss end-of-life issues with the residents, and an arts programme to serve the children in the estate.

In this way, CRT members said they benefitted from learning about the life stories of the residents, their needs, and other aspects of the intrinsic value. Lim and Ng also discuss how to overcome the scepticism of formal government and social agencies they encountered as a collection of volunteers.

The CFT's appeal for the future is that citizen groups like them to be treated as "equal partners in shaping the social space" through more open and transparent exchange of information between the state and civic actors. It would also be indicated by the extent to which they are treated as "legitimate contributors" to policy discussions because of the valuable community knowledge that have acquired and not the hands and legs that deliver alternative services. This is how the fourth generation of leaders can help to make civic action effective and sustainable even as younger citizens such as CRT wish to form communities of care.

Informal but committed groups of active citizens are formulating what it means to belong to the community and country; defining what "nation" means through their concern, practical acts of care, thoughtful reflection and even imagination of a better future.

In this volume, we see the role and efficacy of grand narrative, critical questioning, alternative visions, strategy, and also ground-up problem-solving, social networking and the uncovering of collective assets among "ordinary citizens" in fostering that sense of belonging and identity with "Singapore".

The essays record the views of thoughtful citizens and friends of the country which will have made an impact when they were first published but we believe make an equally significant contribution when compiled together in this way. Through them we not only hear common concerns about our strength as a nation, but also a unity of purpose and an uncommon hope for a brighter and better future.

At a time when the belief in shared prosperity among nations is waning, when the idea of cooperation for the common global good seems naïve, we hope that a dose of ideas and ideals about our Little Red Dot from these past essays can give us the steel to prevail within, and even some inspiration for others to do the same among those beyond our shores.

Arts, Culture and Identity

Chapter 1

Struggling over the Arts and the Artist in Singapore*

Terence Chong

*This article was originally published in Commentary, Volume 21 titled "A Portrait of the Arts in Singapore" © 2012 The National University of Singapore Society. Dr Terence Chong is Director (Research Division) and Deputy Chief Executive Officer of the ISEAS – Yusof Ishak Institute.

In the arts, as with everything else, the struggle for power comes in a variety of forms. Of these, the one over meaning is probably the most dynamic. After all, when it comes to the control of public funds or the flexing of regulatory muscle, local arts groups have to contend with an uneven playing field where the state reigns supreme. It is, however, in the struggle for the meaning of Art and the role of the Artist that the contest becomes more open and because of this, more overt.

The tug-of-war between states and artists over the meaning of Art is endless as it is global. The more salient issue is the particular values and meanings inserted, sometimes surreptitiously, sometimes less so, into notions of Art by states and artists alike for they are sharp indications of respective interests as well as their economic and political positions in society. This article looks at the way the Singapore state has harnessed the arts and culture for a "civilised" and "cultured" society, an ideological site for fantasies of multiracialism and the different roles of the Artist as championed by the state as well as artists themselves.

The Arts for a New Society

The Singapore grand narrative is that of an island-state forced by political and geographical circumstances to hinge its national survival on economic growth. Through astute leadership and hard work, the nation has overcome the odds to enjoy the trappings of a first world country. It is a narrative that does not revere the arts. A typical assessment would read something like this, "During the 1960s and 1970s, while the government focused on the country's economic development and its citizens concerned themselves with ensuring that their proverbial rice bowls remained full, Singapore was not known as a country with its own distinct national tradition in the arts".[1]

This lack of a "distinct national tradition" however, did not mean that the People's Action Party (PAP) Government was slow to grasp

[1] Peterson, William, *Theatre and the Politics of Culture in Contemporary Singapore* (Connecticut: Wesleyan University Press, 2001), 1.

the opportunities that the arts and culture offered to the nation-building project. Indeed, the history of the arts and culture in Singapore cannot be told without the state in the protagonist role.

There was no one nimbler than S Rajaratnam, Singapore's first Minister of Culture, in not only *elevating* but also *exploiting* the Artist for ideological ends. In 1964, with Singapore still part of Malaysia, he noted that:

> The great artist is one who can see what is universal and permanent in what to the untrained eye is particular and transitory. Perhaps Malaysian artists can help us to see what is permanent and universal in Malaysia where ordinary people only see a diversity of races, religion, language, customs and habits. The Malaysian view, after all, is one where what we have in common is more important than our differences. The non-communal view of the Malaysian artist can do a great deal to accelerate the growth of a Malaysian consciousness.[2]

The reluctant birth of the Singapore nation less than a year later made the artist's gift for the "universal and permanent" all the more urgent in the newly formed polyglot society. The arts enjoyed a rudimentary relationship to culture in the eyes of PAP leaders. "The arts" as the production of conventional artefacts like paintings, theatre, music and literature were seen as signifiers of "culture", generally defined by the state as a prescribed set of social practices and pseudo-ethnic values. The unquestioned naturalness of these signifiers explored below, were particularly critical given the pressing need to create a new Singaporean society upon Independence, as well as the PAP Government's highly essentialist and ontological perspectives on "race" and its determination of an individual's "culture" and "heritage".

[2]Rajaratnam, S., speech by the Minister of Culture at the Opening of the Art Exhibition Organised by the Joint Committee of the Singapore Malay Organisations, November 12, 1964, 5.30pm, National Library.

Creating "Civilised" and "Cultivated" Citizens

> It is through Art, and through Art only, that we can realize our perfection; through Art and Art only that we can shield ourselves from the sordid perils of actual existence.[3]

It is unlikely that Wilde was ever prerequisite bedtime reading for the PAP ruling elite but they certainly shared the playwright's moral aestheticism. For one, the PAP Government saw traditional forms of high art as a means to ennoble the soul and to create a society that was "civilised" and "cultured", with the dichotomy between "high culture" and other forms of "lower" popular culture clear and unproblematic. Good art was a vehicle for the very best that "culture" had to offer, which was said to be the "pursuit of our total perfection" and "the best which has been thought and said in the world".[4]

Just like every medicine needs a good disease, the familiar complaint that Singaporeans were dedicated solely to materialism while lacking refinement is a perennial one ripe for the arts antidote. Way back in 1964, Yusof Ishak, later to become Singapore's first President, observed that "for it used to be a common slander in the old days, that while the people of Malaysia, and in particular Singapore, are good at making money, they're indifferent to the finer graces of civilised life".[5] Echoing the same sentiments, Senior Minister of State for Foreign Affairs Rahim Ishak, opined in 1977 that "Art generally can help make our domestic lives that much more pleasant and agreeable. Some of us become embarrassed when we are called "ugly Singaporeans". Lack of appreciation of the arts is a contributory factor to this phenomenon."[6] These complaints of uncouth

---

[3] Wilde, Oscar, *The Critic as Artist* (California: Green Integer, 1997).

[4] Arnold, Matthew, *Culture and Anarchy: An Essay in Political and Social Criticism* (Middlesex: The Echo Library, 2008 [1869]), 5.

[5] Ishak, Yusof, speech by His Excellency the Yang Di-Pertuan Negara at the Opening of the Singapore Art Society's 15th Annual Exhibition, April 23, 1964, 5.30pm, Victoria Memorial Hall.

[6] Ishak, Rahim, "Art and Gracious Living," in *Speeches: A Monthly Collection of Ministerial Speeches* 1(7) (Jan) (Singapore: Ministry of Culture, 1978).

Singaporeans were recurring tropes in government discourse and were the precursor to Goh Chok Tong's lamentations of a "parvenu society", the solution to which, then and now, were the arts and culture.

It was thus poetic that the most morally instructive advice on how to write the Great Singapore Play came from an economist. At a PAP Bukit Merah variety show at the Victoria Theatre on 7 April 1967, Deputy Prime Minister and Minister for Defence, Dr Goh Keng Swee took time off from his busy schedule to divulge the following formula. "Firstly, the themes of the plays should be in keeping with the realistic life in Singapore and its multi-racial, multi-cultural and multi-religious spirit. Secondly, they must discard the crazy, sensual, ridiculous, boisterous and over materialistic style of the West. In the same way, the feudalistic, superstitious, ignorant and pessimistic ideas of the East are also undesirable. Thirdly, they must emphasise the spirit of patriotism, love for the people and for sciences, and cultivate diligence, courage, sense of responsibility and a positive philosophy of life. Fourthly, they must be free from crudeness in production, opportunism, monotony, vulgarity, copying and backwardness. Fifthly, they should provide noble, healthy and proper cultural entertainment for the people".[7] His instructions summoned the spirit of Soviet Socialist Realism which demanded that the artist produce truthful and realistic representations of life as a vehicle for the ideological transformation of society.

A Site for "Multiracial" Fantasies

> In our society, where we place value on the pragmatic and the possible, the social soil is likely to be favourable to the growth of an art-style that is at once a reflection of the Republic's multi-racial life-style. In such a society, art for art's sake has less meaning.[8]

[7] Goh, Keng Swee, speech by the Minister of Defence at the PAP Bukit Merah Variety Show, April 7, 1967, Victoria Theatre.

[8] Chan, Chee Seng, speech by the Parliamentary Secretary (Social Affairs) at the Occasion of the Opening of the "Art for Everyone" Exhibition, July 9, 1971, 8pm, Maude Road Community Centre.

One concrete way in which the arts were exploited for ideological ends was in the state's efforts to spread the "multiracial" messages. According to Benjamin, "The term "culture" is used more and more to refer only to the sort of projective fantasies that can be performed on stage or written in books, and less and less to the patterns that lie behind the contemporary everyday life of ordinary Singaporeans".[9] Culture, as interpreted by the PAP ruling elite, was closely intertwined with notions of civilisation and ethnic traditions. This link is easily made because of the ruling party's insistence on the prevailing importance of a person's "race" to his or her values, socio-cultural habits and world view. Or as a senior government official put it succinctly, "Thus if one is a Chinese, or a Malay, or an Indian, being a part of his society, he must live within the world of his particular culture".[10] It was this close relationship between the arts and ethnic culture that allowed the government to play out its multiracial fantasies.

To this end, especially in the early years, the arts were "culturally symbolic expressions of communal identity associated with the more popular practice of the traditional arts (for example, Chinese music or opera, Indian dance, Malay drama, and Western ballet)" and this was "collectively the approved expression of an instant Singapore multicultural identity".[11] This "instant Singapore multicultural identity" was typically performed in spaces like schools, community centres, and the annual National Day Parades. A representative multiracial performance would comprise children or adults of the three main "races" — Chinese, Malay and Indian — dressed in their

---

[9] Benjamin, Geoffrey, "The Cultural Logic of Singapore's Multiculturalism," in *Singapore: Society in Transition*, ed. Riaz Hassan (Kuala Lumpur: Oxford University Press, 1976), 122.

[10] Ismail, Ghazali, talk by the Political Secretary to the Ministry of Education on "Malay Cultural Contribution to Singapore's Tourist Industry", December 7, 1969, 6pm, Cultural Centre.

[11] Koh, Tai Ann, "Culture and the Arts," in *Management of Success: The Moulding of Modern Singapore*, eds. Sandhu, Kernial, and Wheatley, Paul (Singapore: Institute of Southeast Asian Studies, 1989), 716.

respective traditional ethnic costumes, meaning the *qipao* for Chinese, the *sarong kebaya* for the Malay and the *sari* for the Indian. The music of cultural performances would characteristically be from instruments popularly associated with the different "race" such as the *erhu* (Chinese), the *kompang* (shallow Malay drum made from cow hide), or the sitar (Indian). Other symbolic expressions of "race" also included the Chinese lion dance, the Malay Tarian Melayu or *joget* and the Indian classical *Bharatanatyam.* All of these were instantly recognisable to local audiences as neat and self-evident representations of distinct "race" categories slowly dancing their way, in deep allegorical bliss, towards racial harmony.

Such performances were, and still are, useful in homogenising and essentialising the broad array of ethnic groups. The Hokkiens, Teochews, Cantonese, and Hakkas were conveniently reduced to "Chinese", while the Bugis, Minangkabaus, Boyanese, Orang Selat, Javanese, and so on were summed up as "Malay", and the Malayalee, Sindhi and Tamil communities seen as "Indian". This reduction of ethnic diversity to the rather more opaque "Chinese-Malay-Indian-Others (CMIO)" categories amounted to the "disciplining of race" for administrative and political expediency.[12]

State-Artist Relations: Lessons from the Renaissance

As the arts were harnessed for state interests, the prescribed position of the Artist began to take shape in the early 1980s. Finance Minister Hon Sui Sen, at the opening of the Third Singapore Arts Festival on 10 December 1980, evoked the example of Renaissance Italy. According to Hon:

> While it may sound romantic for artists to starve and work in their garrets, the output of such artists without patronage must be

[12] Purushotam, Nirmala, "Disciplining Difference: 'Race' in Singapore," in *Southeast Asian Identities: Culture and the Politics of Representation in Indonesia, Malaysia, Singapore, and Thailand,* ed. Kahn, Joel (New York: St. Martin's Press, 1998).

> abysmally low. A Michelangelo could not have given of his best without the beneficence of a Pope Sixtus with a Sistine Chapel to be decorated: Neither could other artists of the Renaissance have done their work without the patronage of princes whose vanity must be flattered or wealth displayed.[13]

Hon's point was that the production of the arts must be closely aligned with systems of patronage of either the private sector or state variety. Four years later in 1984, Minister for Foreign Affairs and Culture, S Dhanabalan, took up the Renaissance trope again. In contrasting the Romantic Movement against the Renaissance, Dhanabalan observed that:

> There is, among some cultured circles today, a most strange conception of the artist and of the patrons of art. Since the Romantic Movement of the early nineteenth century, the notion has developed that a true artist is a free spirit, even a rebel against society, a Bohemian often with unsavoury habits, and a visionary with long hair and wild eyes, doing whatever he is inspired to do...This is considered the ideal world of art and culture.[14]

He went on to assert that:

> The Renaissance world was quite different. In the Renaissance world and for much of Western history, the artist was often considered a craftsman. The artist did not consider it demeaning to be working to meet the demands of his patron within the bounds set by his patron...This is not to say that he just did what he was told. But his inspiration and creativity could not run too far ahead of his patrons.[15]

---

[13] Hon, Sui Sen, "Festival of Arts Must Involve Entire Community," in *Speeches: A Monthly Collection of Ministerial Speeches* 4(7) (Jan) (Singapore: Ministry of Culture, 1978), 2.

[14] Dhanabalan, S., "Artists Have to Depend on Patronage," in *Speeches: A Monthly Collection of Ministerial Speeches* 8(1) (Jan/Feb) (Singapore: Ministry of Culture, 1984), 32.

[15] Ibid, 32–33.

For Dhanabalan, the Singapore Artist was no different from any other worker who had to abide by the wishes of his employer. As a craftsman, the artist could and *should* work within the perimeters set by the Singapore state. Unlike Raja's Artist, who was able to see beyond the "particular and transitory", Dhana's Artist found himself (invariably masculine in the eyes of the state) firmly and specifically embedded within a hierarchical order.

In 2000, the Renaissance theme was revived yet again with the publication of the *Renaissance City Report*. This time, the political relationship between state and artist was de-emphasised. Instead, the promotion of the city-state as a cultural hub and the need to dissuade mobile Singaporeans from emigrating led policy makers to highlight the multiple talents of the "Renaissance Singaporean". The "Renaissance Singaporean", according to the *Renaissance Report* in typically gendered language, is "an individual with an open, analytical and creative mind that is capable of acquiring, sharing, applying and creating new knowledge" while "attuned to his Asian roots and heritage".[16] Such pronouncements were in keeping with the Government's practice of legitimising specific constructions of the Singapore Artist by emptying universally recognised concepts of their historical significance and filling them up with state-friendly meaning and values.

The Singapore Artist as Deviant

In prescribing the Artist's role, the state was also apt at exploiting archetypal artistic biographies. These biographies are usually syncretic concoctions of artistic stereotypes, a constructed life-script that submits artists to convenient objectification infused with local political interests and values. One widely recognisable biography of the Artist is that of the "deviant". As scripts of hedonism, self-indulgence and self-gratification, such biographies are useful in

[16] Ministry of Information and the Arts, *Renaissance City Report: Culture and the Arts in Renaissance Singapore* (Singapore: Ministry of Information and the Arts, 2000).

raising moral panic and consequently, justification for greater regulation.

"Deviance" is no more evident than in the "conflation of artist with the homosexual in Singapore".[17] The greater tolerance of sexual minorities in the arts community has led to its crystallisation as a homogenous site of gay identities, thus underlining it as a location of "sexual deviance" or as "aberrant, anti-social and/or immoral".[18] In 1994, Josef Ng, a performance artist, snipped off his pubic hair at a New Year show organised by The 5th Passage before a small audience in symbolic protest against police entrapment of gays. At the same show, Shannon Tham, another performance artist, vomited into a bucket as part of his performance, also in protest of gay entrapment. Ng was fined S$1,000 for committing an obscene act. The local media had a field day, prompting the National Arts Council (NAC) to issue a public statement saying that "NAC finds the acts vulgar and completely distasteful, which deserve public condemnation. By no stretch of the imagination can such acts be construed and condoned as art. Such acts, in fact, debase art and lower the public's esteem for art and artists in general".[19] Episodes like these reinforce the notion of the Singapore Government as stern parent "'putting up' with the hyperactive, overly imaginative artist-child. If the artist-child becomes 'unmanageable', an embarrassment in public, he must be disciplined and 'sent to his room without dinner', that is, removed from the scene — naturally, it is all done for his own good".[20]

---

[17] Seet, K. K., "Interpellation, Ideology and Identity: The Case of Talaq," *Theatre Research International* 27, no. 2 (2002): 157.

[18] Heng, Russell Hiang Khng, "Tiptoe Out of the Closet: The Before and After of the Increasingly Visible Gay Community in Singapore," in *Gay and Lesbian Asia*, eds. Sullivan, Gerard, and Jackson, Peter (New York: Harrington Press, 2001), 88; Lo, Jacqueline, *Staging Nation: English Language Theatre in Malaysia and Singapore* (Hong Kong: Hong Kong University Press, 2004), 121.

[19] Lee, Weng Choy, "Chronology of a Controversy," http://www.biotechnics.org/Chronology%20of%20a%20controversy.htm.

[20] Sasitharan, Thirunalan, "The Arts: Of Swords, Harnesses and Blinkers," in *State-Society Relations in Singapore*, eds. Koh, Gillian, and Ooi, Geok Ling (Singapore: Eastern Universities Press, 2003), 137–138.

Deviant biographies are not always state imposed. In some cases, they are claimed by artists themselves. Elangovan, playwright and artistic director of Agni Koothu (Theatre of Fire), springs to mind. Known for provocative works which "often explore the untouched realities and impotency of the Tamil minority in Singapore", he "believes that art should conscientize [sic], confront and question accepted societal stereotypes of vision, perception, feeling and judgment to examine reality as a historical and social process".[21] His plays are characterised by expletives and crude language, and he has even resorted to locking auditorium doors to prevent his audience from leaving, flouting safety regulations. Some have argued that "Elangovan sees the dramatist as a kind of *agent provocateur* and construes the artistic behaviour as necessarily challenging the status quo".[22] Most famous for his plays *Talaq* (1999) and *Smegma* (2006), both of which address religion in a controversial manner, Elangovan and his wife, S Themoli, have an astute understanding of the local media's relationship with local theatre, and have been highly successful in leveraging the media and its interests for exposure and attention.[23]

The Singapore Artist as Prometheus

Two of the most enduring ingredients of the Artist's biography are Truth and Suffering. They legitimise each other, marking the Artist as the outsider who is willing, dedicated and altruistic. Like Prometheus who defied the gods to bring fire to enlighten the lives of mortals only to suffer the ignominy of having birds pick at his liver for all eternity, the Artist too must embrace Truth and Suffering as one and the same. Although universal, it is amidst the landscapes of hegemony and dominant ideology in illiberal regimes where this biography stands out.

---

[21] Elangovan. 1999. Talaq. Singapore: Elangovan, 93.

[22] Seet, "Interpellation," 154.

[23] Ibid.

The Singapore political landscape has been fertile ground. The fate of The Third Stage, a political English-language theatre group formed in the early-1980s, is one such example. From its very first production, *Cry for a Cactus* (1983) that explored the constraints of compulsory National Service, *Oh Singapore!* (1985) on the interventionist state, to *Esperanza* (1987) on the plight of exploited Filipina maids, the theatre group quickly established a reputation for unvarnished portrayals of marginal communities. Its amateurish production values lent precious authenticity to its drama at a time of strong economic growth and an expanding middle class. All this came to an abrupt end with the so-called "Marxist conspiracy" in 1987. A total of 22 individuals from different walks of life were accused of plotting, behind the veil of the Catholic Church's "liberation theology", to overthrow the Government. As part of Operation Spectrum, Wong Souk Yee and Chng Suan Tze, members of The Third Stage were also detained. The "political play" that the Third Stage was known for — guerilla-like, low in production values, politically confrontational and socially pointed, issue-driven, underlined with a clear ideological orientation — faded into oblivion.

The best known of such biographies is perhaps that of the late Kuo Pao Kun. Born in Hubei, China, moving to Hong Kong, then to Singapore and later Australia, and back again to Singapore, Kuo's life falls neatly into the narrative of the outsider-heterodox artist. Kuo's activism in left-wing Chinese-language theatre led to his detention without trial under the Internal Security Act in 1976. His release in 1980 came with restrictions on residence and travel until 1983 while his Singapore citizenship, revoked in 1977, was only restored in 1994. Indeed, Kuo's biography may be discursively read as the archetypal heterodox artist who challenged state orthodoxies over social justice and cultural ideology while never relinquishing his sense of humanity even after incarceration. Certainly, Kuo himself understood the need for the artistic *habitus* to be seen as an outsider because "I think that kind of marginality, a fringe kind of experience, allows one to compare and reflect".[24] Indeed, Kuo's

[24] Kuo, Pao Kun, "Between Two Worlds: A Conversation with Kuo Pao Kun," in *9 Lives: 10 Years of Singapore Theatre: Essays Commissioned by The Necessary Stage* (Singapore: First Printers, 1997).

work is often presented by his peers and admirers as deeply reflective of the Singapore postcolonial condition not because it is mainstream but for the artist's ability to produce "images at the margins" of society (Kuo's collection of plays was compiled into a 2000 volume titled *Images at the Margins*).

Inscribed in such biographies are not only the artist's abilities and gifts but also the *right* to challenge dominant ideology and orthodoxies. It is a biography of heterodoxy, always in tension with the norms of society; and one that is well acknowledged by the state. According to Ong Keng Sen, "the official perception of the artist [is] as 'an outsider in Singapore...the other' in the face of materialism and capitalism".[25]

Conclusion

The biographies of artists will continue to be the object of struggle between the state and the artists themselves. On one hand, the dependence of the artistic community on public funds will subject the arts to the political agenda of the state, while on the other, the artistic community's efforts to exercise its autonomy against institutional *de rigueur* is romantic as it is universal. How this struggle will unfold will depend on the controversies which allow such biographies to play out, as well as the personal views of political leaders who will set the tone for the state's response. Indeed, the relatively enlightened positions of individuals like S Rajaratnam and Ong Teng Cheong have encouraged the arts to flourish despite the country's single minded devotion to the economy. Because of their political standing, they have been able to raise the profile of the arts during their tenure. Singapore artists today, like their Renaissance counterparts, could do with powerful patrons.

---

[25] Seet, "Interpellation," 157.

Chapter 2

The Arts, Culture and Singapore as Global City*

C. J. W.-L. Wee

*This article was originally published in Commentary, Volume 21 titled "A Portrait of the Arts in Singapore" © 2012 The National University of Singapore Society. Dr C. J. W.-L. Wee is Professor of English in the Division of English at the Nanyang Technological University, and Fellow at the ISEAS – Yusof Ishak Institute.

Having a population of 5.1 million people, including foreigners, in 2010, Singapore is distinct from other post-colonial societies. In striving to match the achievements of the advanced West, it forsook not only many of the political dimensions of democratic life associated with it but also its cultural dimensions at the level of high-art and in the "way of life" sense. Instead, an industrial and commercial understanding of culture was elevated, and manufacturing and productive institutions became the collective basis of social life. Yet, despite a puritanical modernity, experimental theatre and visual art started to flourish in the 1980s.

Such developments were noticed by the People's Action Party (PAP) state. The 19 July 1999 issue of *Time* asked on its cover: "Singapore swings: Can Asia's nanny state give up its authoritarian ways?". The magazine said, "Culturally, Singapore is permitting artists to stage a range of socially and politically controversial performances."[1] The year 1990 saw the succession of Goh Chok Tong to Prime Minister. This led to policy changes in policy interests including a formulation of cultural policy by the government. The National Arts Council (NAC) was set up in 1991 and the Ministry of Information and the Arts (MITA) was created: a ministry that had "PAP intellectual-in-waiting [George] Yeo in charge. The new minister enthused about fostering a global renaissance city, about making Singaporeans more creative, about forging a civic society...."[2]

It is understood in the city-state though, that the Government has not simply gone humanistically soft. In order to be a "creative economy" and a "happening" global city that can retain competitive business and industrial talent, both foreign and local, Singapore cannot display just pragmatic modernity: New public policies have been set in place to foster artistic creativity and create an arts market, thinking that such creativity would, in turn, encourage technological and entrepreneurial innovation. This newer circumstance poses challenges for the very innovative artistic energy that

[1] McCarthy, Terry, and Ellis, Eric, "Singapore Lightens Up," *Time*, July 19, 1999, 17.
[2] Ibid, 19.

the state wants to foster. This essay explores some of the tensions arising from the recent changes.

Arts Developments in the 1990s

The city-state of Singapore, under PAP's leadership since 1959, represents a capitalist modernity that deliberately forsook autochthony in cultural development for economic success. In a fundamental way, this was the argument that literary critic Koh Tai Ann made of the Singapore state's approach to cultural matters from the early years of Independence to the late 1980s, when "culture" was used for the central purpose of nation-building.[3] Since then, it has been open to creating a cultural superstructure that would match its status as a major regional financial and industrial hub. "Culture", in the 20-odd years prior, had referred more to multiethnic cultures and values, though by the 1980s to the mid-1990s, "culture" also signified the mythicised "Asian" values that were the alleged foundation of Singapore's "East-Asian Miracle" status. Cultural policy — policy that fostered the arts and high culture — was not a priority. The PAP's reputation for forging a conventional society composed mainly of shopping centres by and large stemmed from a pragmatic, petit-bourgeois vision of a hardworking modern society.

By 1989, a recognisable cultural policy started to be articulated with the government's *Report of the Advisory Council on Culture and the Arts.*[4] By then, there was already a burgeoning theatre scene led principally by The Theatre Practice (TTP), The Necessary Stage (TNS) and TheatreWorks (Singapore). There was also a nascent and experimental visual arts development. Before we can assess the impact of official arts policy on the contemporary arts, it is necessary

---

[3] Koh, Tai Ann, "Culture and the Arts," in *The Management of Success: The Moulding of Modern Singapore*, eds. Sandhu, Kernial, and Wheatley, Paul (Singapore: Institute of Southeast Asian Studies, 1989).

[4] Ong, Teng Cheong *et al.*, *Report of the Advisory Council on Culture and the Arts* (Singapore: Singapore National Printers, 1989).

to have some sense of these artistic emergences and their relationship to official culture.

In theatre, TTP's Kuo Pao Kun was the major enabling personality. He had been detained without trial by the state between 1976–80 for alleged communist activities. Kuo returned in the 1980s with plays that examined both the severe weakening of culture and cultural memory in the wake of a state-led modernisation, and held out the possibility of trans-ethnic understanding. He broke the mould of single-language theatre with plays such as the now iconic *Mama Looking for Her Cat* (1988) that used Mandarin, Hokkien, English and Tamil. Kuo was a natural institution builder, able to generously support younger talent. He harnessed the energy of visual artists involved with newer arts practices such as performance art — introduced to Singapore by visual artist and Fukuoka Cultural Prize winner Tang Da Wu — and pioneered an emerging multidisciplinary contemporary arts scene.

The three companies created adventurous theatre productions, often formally bold, with scripts created in a workshop setting, dealing with issues of memory, ethnic and other identity issues in works like *Rosnah* (1996) and *Pillars* (1997). These were artistic reactions against the singular and top-down disciplinary modernisation of Singapore since the mid-1960s which did not really foster space for reflection on cultural or historical issues. As part of the dynamic process of experimenting with theatre form in relation to Singapore identity in the 1980's to mid-1990's, "difficult" theatre became the mainstream of the theatre groups; this theatre even co-existed with indigenised Broadway-style musicals within the companies. Gender issues were noticeable by the early 1990s in works like *Lest the Demons* (1992), *Private Parts* (1992), and *Mergers and Accusations* (1995). Whatever the shortcomings were of early professionalism in theatre, they were invigorating years.

In the visual arts, the return of Tang Da Wu from London in 1988 (after the best part of 20 years in England) led to his founding of a community called the Artists' Village in 1989, in an abandoned village in then-rural Sembawang. This ruralism was also a critique of the petit-bourgeois urban society that Singapore was becoming.[5] Another visual-art collective that emerged was the 5th Passage group, linked with Susie Lingham and Suzanne Victor, which functioned until 1994.[6]

The contemporary and anti-commercial art that arrived with Tang was eclectic. There were dynamic and energising experiments in conceptual art, performance, installation sculpture that used pre-existing or "found objects", figurative painting that had German expressionist antecedents (but executed with personal rather than historical references), pop art and "happenings". There had been earlier intimations of such artistic possibilities, but they were just that — intimations. The various ethnicities of the predominantly younger artists Tang mentored also made for a challenging experimentation with themes that implicitly or otherwise engaged the state's wished-for bland identity and urban modernity. The environment, sexuality, gendered, feminism and other forms of identity became areas for enquiry. The world of abstract modern art of the 1970s was largely transformed. Many artists were from less-privileged and often non-English-speaking social strata, which distinguished them from the more bourgeois background of English-language theatre practitioners, providing a distinctive edge to the visual arts. The overall creative release brought critical judgement into the aesthetic realm.

The 1980s to the early 1990s' flourishing of the arts was, to some extent, possible because of the favoured pragmatic-philistine modernity. Singapore society, in its mercantile/industrial indifference to humanistic endeavour, gave space for artistic growth. The year 1987, though, was a hard one for theatre. A predominantly English-

---

[5] In 1989, Tang is quoted as saying that: "The main reason for being here [in Sembawang] is the isolation." The magazine writer's response to this was: "The psychological context of the village is earthy, rudimentary, and free of the numerous and trivial distractions normally found in the city" (Chia, Ming Chien, "The Artists' Village," *Man* (April-May 1989), 33).

[6] Susie Lingham, "A Quota on Expression: Visions, Vexations and Vanishings — Contemporary Art in Singapore from the Late 1980s to the Present," in *Negotiating Home, History and Nation: Two Decades of Contemporary Art in Southeast Asia 1881–2011*, exhibition catalogue (Singapore: Singapore Art Museum, 2011).

language group called the Third Stage that had addressed social problems — Filipino maids in the city-state, among them — was affected by government action taken against what was described as a Marxist conspiracy, one that affected not only the theatre practitioners but also Roman-Catholic social workers. The space opened up again for theatre thereafter, until another high-profile controversy at the end of 1993 — this time, unexpectedly, centred on the arts alone. The immediate causes for this were a number of performance arts events and experiments in contemporary theatre. A visual artist undertook urine-drinking as part of his performance. Soon after, a 21-year-old performance artist and Augusto Boal-style Forum Theatre practised by TNS were accused, respectively, of obscenity and having a Marxist orientation. The latter charge which coincided with the collapse of the Berlin Wall, sounded odd to some ears.[7]

Performance art remained officially in a position of limbo and could not receive NAC funding until the ban was effectively lifted in 2003. Despite these obstacles, the desire for a commodified arts scene has since escalated.

What is curious is a sort of "backwards" arts development. There was, first, an experimental arts scene, which was *then* followed by attempts to increase the necessary infrastructure of proper arts education in the schools, major art spaces or museums (the Singapore Art Museum, for example, was opened only in 1996), and major theatre venues (the large part of the 1990s saw only "black box" venues being opened; the other options remained the inappropriately large Kallang Theatre — now closed — and the colonial-era Victoria Theatre).

In 1992, the policy to make the city-state not only a Global City, but indeed, a Global City for the Arts was launched. As is often the case in Singapore, an "it-needs-to-transpire-tomorrow" approach was adopted for the new cultural policy. The entrenched position of this

[7] For more information and documentation of the events, see Krishnan, Sanjay, Kuttan, Sharaad, Lee, Weng Choy, Perera, Leon, and Yap, Jimmy (eds.), *Looking at Culture* (Singapore: Artres Design & Communications, 1996).

paradigm, we will see, gives rise to the central tension between the professed wish for a dynamic creativity and an instrumental-rational mental set.

Arts funding increased and theatre, as the most visible art form, was a major beneficiary. The awkwardly titled *Renaissance City Report: Culture and the Arts in Renaissance Singapore* (2000)[8] advocated more funding be made available (some S$50 million over five years) and these funds have since made a noticeable impact on the cultural scene. In infrastructural terms, the crowning development was the October 2002 opening of the S$600-million "Esplanade — Theatres on the Bay" arts complex. The Esplanade was criticised for not being a venue supportive of local theatre development given that it had no medium-sized theatre space: its major theatre auditorium seats some 1,800 persons — a number that both the older and newer theatre companies would find daunting to fill.

How the arts will develop in the new millennium depends primarily on the artists themselves but the quality of the environment set up by the state in support of their endeavours is important. Within the ambit of what is called "globalisation", cultural policy worldwide increasingly recognises the economic importance of the creative arts such as film, video, new media, broadcasting and so on. The Government understands these trends well. While it is possible that aesthetic values might be replaced by the commercial values of the market place, we can also see the new media as offering an expansion of creative possibilities. For these possibilities to be realised, it is imperative that a fundamental point be recognised: *that the arts lie at the core of the cultural sector, and creativity as a process is at the core of the arts.* There needs to be more of a marked shift in thinking from the older, entrenched form of a disciplinary, economics-oriented instrumental-rationality if profound artistic heights are to be achieved. The relevant factor simply may be: *more autonomy.*

The late Kuo Pao Kun in 1999 argued in *The Arts Magazine* (the now-defunct magazine of The Esplanade) that the 1990s had been

[8] Ministry of Information and the Arts, *Renaissance City Report: Culture and the Arts in Renaissance Singapore* (Singapore: Ministry of Information and the Arts, 2000).

good for the arts — new artists and creative groups; more commercial galleries; more festivals; and, importantly, more young people "plunged into the arts profession". However, he noted:

> "Directly and indirectly, the state and its numerous agencies control the bulk of the public funding for the arts, all the major performing and exhibition venues and their year round schedule...as well as the underpinning power to censor all public shows.
>
> As the country enters a new millennium with a resolution to become an international arts centre, not to mention its ambition to be part of the Asian Renaissance, this arts regime...appears totally out of date. ..."

Kuo added that:

> "While it is true that such infrastructures can and do provide opportunities, state management has been generally suffocating in spirit....Instead, the arts, as a dimension functionally distinct from politics and economics, deserves its own autonomous space above institutional politics because original and creative expressions always shoot up from the ground and are inclined to evoke longer philosophic vision, larger intellectual perspectives and more radical aesthetics venturing beyond the status quo."[9]

Kuo also made reference to 1993. The fundamental problem, he observes, may be that the government is concerned mainly to nurture an arts market or industry rather than the arts *per se.* If this is true, then

> "Singapore is short changing itself. Controlled innovation programmes and managed innovative arts industries are useful additions to its economy....But Singaporeans deserve the full flowering of the arts, as they deserve the full spectrum of creative thinking. Not to do so is to under-rate the people's intellectual and intuitive potentials, to deny them the opportunity to make primary

---

[9] Kuo, Pao Kun, "Re-Positioning the Arts," *The Arts Magazine* (November/December 1999), 19–20.

contributions. Primary and Original — these are key concepts in the world of Art and Creativity."[10]

In fact, one might add, "controlled innovation" may even stanch the creativity necessary for the knowledge-based industries and cultural industries that we want for our competitive, post-industrial economic future.

In many ways, though, what Kuo enunciated chimed with the findings of the Singapore 21 Committee, as published by the Government in *Singapore 21: Together, We Make the Difference.* The report noted that a survey done in 1998 "found only 15% of Singaporeans willing to contribute to their community".[11] Three recurring themes helped explain this lack: first, no sense of ownership over the issues the citizenry face; second, no sense of respect accorded to the citizenry; and third, no trust for the citizenry. The artistic section of Singapore's national community, thus, are part of a representative sociological sample of opinion. In terms of an emerging and active civil society, it can be said that artists are willing to make their citizenship count through their participation in making (in Kuo's phrase) "primary contributions" to their society.

The general solution *Singapore 21* advances is "active citizenship", an idea "as old as the idea of democracy itself": "We will benefit from greater responsiveness, more consultation and a wider range of views and ideas. The crux is how to do so without losing the efficiency, decisiveness and collective [state] action that has enabled Singaporeans to thrive."[12] This is perhaps the rub. It takes us back to Kuo's claim that while the arts represent a realm "functionally distinct from politics and economics", it nevertheless will evoke "perspectives…venturing beyond the status quo".

In the long term, it is best not to see more "active citizenship" as the loss of efficiency and decisive state action, but as the *means* by

---

[10] Ibid, 22.

[11] Government of Singapore, *Singapore 21: Together, We Make the Difference* (Singapore: Singapore 21 Committee, 1999), 49.

[12] Ibid, 51, 50.

which the nation will be able both to survive and thrive within an era of globalisation.

The Arts and the Instrumentalisation of Culture

I mentioned earlier that the formulation of cultural policy around the world increasingly takes into account the economic potential of cultural industries. The danger, however, of substituting aesthetic and cultural values with commercial values subject to the market place is real, especially in Singapore where these values are arguably still little understood. The policy changes thus far implemented may not spur the arts on effectively, for the general mental set may still be too mired in older forms of instrumental-rationalist thinking. This must be addressed in a more thoroughgoing manner before more trenchant forms of cultural policy on cultural re-generation can result.

The Economic Development Board (EDB, the agency that has contributed so much to the city-state's capitalist success) and MITA's document, *Singapore — Global City for the Arts* (1992), is a representative instance of pragmatism's limits. The document announced the impending arrival of a number of distinct national cultural institutions — mainly to potential overseas investors — such as the Singapore Art Museum and the Singapore History Museum (now the National Museum of Singapore). They are to function in a heritage district: "[The Museum Precinct's] importance is underscored by its site in the heart of the Civic District, an area rich in history. Five museums will be housed in this precinct, linked by commercial complexes and surface and underground passages"; further, "[i]t is our hope that Singapore will be a centre of culture in East Asia".[13]

When one looks carefully at the Overview, a number of concerns can be raised: "Singapore, who draws her energies from the dynamics of her multi-cultural population, is plugged into the network of

[13] Economic Development Board and Ministry of Information and the Arts, *Singapore — Global City for the Arts* (Singapore: Economic Development Board and Ministry of Information and the Arts, 1992), 11, 3.

cultural capitals. She aims to be a global city for the arts by 1999."[14] Apart from the fact that 1999 has passed, the text erroneously suggests that high culture can be produced in the same way as a printed circuit board, and according to a timetable. What sort of qualitative performance indicators would one use, in any case, to measure the arrival of Singapore at the status of the London of Southeast Asia, save for pure figures on how many art auctions were held here, given that Singapore has become a regional centre for art auctions, fairs and exhibitions?

The Overview then announces the economic assumptions behind the document: "Where the Republic once forged a reputation in trade, manufacturing, financial and service industries, she is now setting the stage for an arts industry to thrive."[15] Singapore's history of social engineering as the basis for nation-building is present here: we have the technology, we have the means, this history says. Then-EDB Chairman Philip Yeo is quoted: "There is now in Singapore a major opportunity to develop the arts, not only for cultural enrichment, but also in the interest of economic growth."[16] No one can take issue with that; but the leap from "cultural enrichment" to "economic growth" occurs in too rapid a step.

The section on "Arts Training" does announce the "software" — more arts training, grants and scholarships — that the relevant state agencies will put in place to support this new enterprise.[17] The existence of new supporting institutions (such as the School of the Arts which was established in 2006) represents an improvement from the past.

While it would be untenable to contend that the arts occupy a space free from the processes of commodification — one Japanese specialist notes, "Since the arts and media make up a major part of the [Japanese] media programme, media policy will feature prominently in cultural policy development. The notion of cultural

[14] Ibid, 3.

[15] Ibid.

[16] Ibid.

[17] Ibid, 21.

development for the sake of culture is increasingly difficult to maintain"[18] — it would *equally* be a misconception to think that the arts can flourish if commercial utility is to be the main driving force. While such an argument in Singapore, or anywhere else, is hardly new, it is made in relation to the city-state's current goal to be a cultural hub. Singapore may instead become an empty hub for other people's high or popular/mass culture to pass through. This will not serve former Prime Minister Goh's goal of making Singapore a "world-class home" in which "Singaporeans want to stay" rather than to emigrate.[19]

The major stumbling block for Singapore — simultaneously a major cause of our economic success and the retardation of cultural progress — is its own history of successful developmentalism. Singapore's post-Independence experience of cultural development has been at variance with the experience not only of Western European, but also of many post-colonial Latin American, African and Asian countries. States took on the responsibility for maintaining material and immaterial historical heritage and in the process, they differentiated themselves from other nations. In many of the plural societies the colonial powers constructed, a "national" heritage was built up through the culture of their élite, which sometimes was of European origin. Modern institutions, such as museums and university departments of study engaging with the new nation's culture, were developed and historical sites maintained in order to strengthen national identity. Supporting ethnic arts and crafts were also part of these strategies as was support for the modern arts (literature, music, the plastic arts) and the mass media. Debates arose over how the urban centre and the provincial periphery, the mod-

---

[18] Watanabe, Michihiro, "Cultural Policies in Japan," in *Culture, Creativity and Markets: World Culture Report 1998*, United Nations Educational, Scientific and Cultural Organization (Paris: United Nations Educational, Scientific and Cultural Organization, 1998), 174.

[19] Ibrahim, Zuraidah, "Singapore's new goal: Be a world-class home: Besides building first-class economy, excellence in education, arts, sports and culture is also important," *The Straits Times*, August 23, 1999.

ern and the traditional, were to be reconciled in such multi-level support of a national identity. But whatever differences were expressed, the idea of the "national culture" dominated, and the state played a leading role in developing.

Nation-building in Singapore, and the PAP government's management of the ethnic fissures in society, took a different route from the more established means of creating the "national" that incorporated cultural policy. "Culture" — particularly the sensitive meanings of "ethnicity" and "race" — was played down. The changes in present cultural policy do not in themselves signify a massive shift in the instrumental-rationalist mentality of nation-building, nor can one realistically expect economically pragmatic thinking that is so successful to disappear overnight. What is pressing, though, is coming to terms with this politico-cultural legacy and its consequences.

The Arts and the Economy in the New Millennium

The contemporary arts scene, since the mid-1990s has seen a normalisation of what were once arts practices with counter-cultural dimensions. What was once unusual is now more standard, or predictable, perhaps. This normalisation in itself is not surprising — it is the pattern in the metropolitan West; what is surprising is the *speed* of the process, having taken place in only about a decade after newer arts practices emerged.

One could say that the state, in some respects, has understood that culture has to a greater or lesser degree become enmeshed with the economy.[20] This is so even as the state still remains true to its older comprehension of the economy as the base of all reality. The strongest challenge to arts development in the new millennium is that it is increasingly becoming part of what might be called "lifestyle capitalism", in which "alternative" socio-cultural stances become co-opted into the diverse cultural mosaic of contemporary cosmopolitanism. Artistic creativity also becomes a part of a desired

[20]Jameson, Fredric, *Postmodernism, or, the Cultural Logic of Late Capitalism* (Durham, NC: Duke University Press, 1991).

less-conformist subjectivity that could drive key sectors of local capitalism.

The state has acknowledged for a number of years that the old Fordist-Taylorised machinery of disciplinary modernisation was starting to creak. The re-shaping of the paradigm began before the 1997 Asian Economic Crisis, though that hastened change; the result is a parading of the buzzwords associated with the "New Economy". However, the entrenched utilitarian-pragmatic mentality of the protective-interventionist state, not surprisingly, plagues the *very ideas* of less-conformist subjectivities and a vibrant socio-cultural life thought to provide the "creative" intellectual and entrepreneurial support for an "Information Society".

In November 1998, then-Prime Minister Goh Chok Tong discussed the recommendations of the Committee on Singapore's Competitiveness. The fundamental policy recommendation was that the island-state must become an advanced knowledge economy in the next decade, with manufacturing and services being the twin engines of growth. A skilful workforce would be needed. Labour and capital become less important than what can be described as "immaterial" labour and "intellectual" capital.[21]

Business, now has less tangible dimensions as to what makes for a remunerative dynamism. *The Straits Times* paraphrased the report thus: "Add some fizz into local entertainment by setting up an Arts Marketplace for interactive arts activities, similar to Melbourne's Sunday Market and Montmartre in Paris. To boost tourism, build more theme parks and study the feasibility of building a new cruise centre."[22] As with the best global versions of metropolitan life, we need to enhance the city-state's stature as a transnational "hub" for the flows of capital. The "hardware", as it is called in Singapore, needs a "software upgrade" — and not only in terms of what can be pragmatically understood like healthcare, or even the environment.

[21] Ibrahim, Zuraidah, "S'pore focus on key areas for growth," *The Straits Times*, October 13, 1998.

[22] "Staying ahead: Business," *The Straits Times*, November 13, 1998.

Singapore at the start of the new millennium had been transformed from a colonial city into a modern if uni-functional premier "world city" with a puritan work ethic, and into an economic centre for business in the Asia-Pacific. The question is whether it can become a multi-functional cultural metropolis, given increased regional and international competition from other aspirational world cities. The need for more autonomy — a need already raised earlier — also applies to artistic and related cultural developments. The city-state has been working out how this freedom and autonomy can be wrought by a state known to believe in discipline.

By 2006, the then-Permanent Secretary of the Ministry of Information, Communications and the Arts (MICA) announced the need for the city-state to have what is these days known as a "re-branding" exercise: "Singapore is seen as a country with a positive brand" and "[i]n tandem with the continual re- invention of the economic and social landscape..., the Singapore 'brand' has shifted from a focus on 'hard' aspects such as costs, efficiency and technology to 'softer' aspects such as lifestyle, experience and innovation."[23] And so, "Sacred cows of the past are being slaughtered with the development of two integrated resorts which will transform our entertainment industry." By "integrated resorts", the writer euphemistically refers to two casino complexes, which are presented along with upmarket shopping and a new art museum (which has now become the ArtScience Museum at Marina Bay Sands). Arts and entertainment are support mechanisms in this newest reinvention of the city-state.

The article next to "Let Us Co-Create Our Nation's Brand" stated that Singapore would host the 2006 annual meetings of the board of governors of the International Monetary Fund and the World Bank Group. All this would take place under the auspices of a larger campaign called Singapore 2006, "Global City, World of Opportunities". The 16,000 delegates would get a taste of Singapore "through various programmes such as the [inaugural] Singapore

[23] Tan, Chin Nam, "Let Us Co-Create Our Nation's Brand," *Fusion@MICA* 10 (April-June 2006).

Biennale 2006".[24] Indeed, the visitor's guide to the Biennale stated that it is the "anchor cultural event"[25] for the meeting. The guide also referred to "Singapore's prominence as an international contemporary arts centre". Such a statement is less surprising now, but in 1993–94, during the arts controversies, this statement would have elicited outright astonishment. International visual arts biennales have become part of the global circulation of high culture. Such art events and also art exhibitions in a similar "globalised" mould have come to operate "within the dimensions of attraction and entertainment, on the one hand, and critical reflection and subversion, on the other".[26]

The state's present development strategy itself is not surprising, given the established pattern of fostering a competitive global city that will lure and retain foreign capital flows. It is the bluntness of its articulation that may catch the reader off-guard. National culture and the arts may become *only* commodities in the process of creating a suitable brand — and of that, we should be careful.

---

[24] "Singapore 2006 Showcases Cosmopolitan Singapore," *Fusion@MICA* 10 (April-June 2006).

[25] *Belief: Singapore Biennale 2006*, 4th September to 12th November 2006, visitor's guide.

[26] Rectanus, Mark W., *Culture Incorporated: Museums, Artists, and Corporate Sponsorships* (Minneapolis: University of Minnesota Press, 2002), 7.

Chapter 3

Still Building*

Alvin Tan

---

*This article was originally published in Commentary, Volume 21 titled "A Portrait of the Arts in Singapore" © 2012 The National University of Singapore Society. Alvin Tan is the Founder of The Necessary Stage and its Artistic Director.

The Building of a Nation

> This country no good. People no good. When I sell food, I wear badge. Smile. I smile.
>
> I go Woodbridge. Got poster. Smile. I smile. I see Woodbridge doctor.
>
> He say how many percent become better, how many percent don't become better.
>
> He smile. I smile. I see social worker.
>
> She say how many percent must take medicine only for few months, how many percent must take always.
>
> If daughter mad, how many percent mother also mad. She smile. I smile.
>
> I go home, I see mirror. I smile. I cannot laugh. I cannot cry. Because I only know how to smile.
>
> I only know how to smile.[1]

In the 1970s, a minister's statement about Singapore being a cultural desert on the front page of a newspaper spurred the nation to embark on a major mission to develop our arts for the future. The Singapore Arts Festival and the annual Drama Festival became regular features on our cultural events calendar. By the 1980s, there were already some fruits to be reaped. The year 1987 saw five new theatre groups formed. They were Action Theatre, Aksens, Arts and Acts, Just Theatre and The Necessary Stage (TNS).

Arts development was then under the Ministry of Community Development (MCD). By 1991, the National Arts Council (NAC) had evolved from MCD, signalling the government's long term vision to develop the arts. In addition to a grant scheme, a Theatre-in-Residence scheme and an Arts Housing scheme were also established and some theatre groups were encouraged to convert their status from societies for companies limited by guarantee to be more accountable to the larger quantum of grants received.

The Theatre-In-Residence Scheme typified the planned social change for arts development in the late 1980s to the early 1990s. Then, Singaporean practitioners tended to either stage foreign

---

[1] Sharma, Haresh, *Off Centre*. Singapore: The Necessary Stage.

plays or adapted them. There were very few original local works. Singaporean directors were not confident enough to develop local scripts. There were a few local playwrights. The notion of having local directors work to develop local scripts with local playwrights was almost non-existent. The Theatre-in-Residence Scheme stipulated that theatre rental would be waived if theatre companies staged four productions a year, two of which had to be original local works. This incentivised theatre companies to change their attitude and behaviour towards local scripts. Over time, directors and theatre companies were rewarded with media attention and a Singaporean audience hungry for local plays. Behavourial change led to an attitudinal change and soon enough, more local plays were written and staged.

Other factors responsible for a nurturing environment were the Shell-NUS Short Play competition and the availability of various lunchtime platforms, namely the NUS, DBS and Shell Lunchtime Performances. Notably, these platforms, which were followed up later by Raw Theatre Festival (The Substation) and Names Changed to Protect the Innocent (TNS), provided incubation environments where young and emerging artists could take risks and experiment with no or little pressure.

In the 1990s, arts development was related to cultural tourism. The Singapore Tourism Board did a survey gathering data on how much people spent when they went out for a play — transport and food — benefiting other industries in the process. This survey helped to justify investing in the arts. It also made Singapore more vibrant and hopefully, less boring to the tourists and/or expatriates working here.

By the late 1990s and early noughties, cultural industries featured large on the global horizon. Singapore started looking at how creativity from the arts could inspire creativity in the other social and economic fields; how design could enhance businesses and investment; and how the arts alone, as entertainment or cutting-edge works, could bring in tourists from all around the world. The arts itself was perceived and valued as a viable industry. That was when Singapore aspired to be an arts hub. With the completion of the Esplanade, Singapore was well-placed to attract foreign artists and therefore increase the diversity in the arts landscape so more tourists would stay longer to the artistic offerings here, rather than just use Singapore as a transit point to other exotic Southeast Asian cities.

With arts hub status, Singapore could also attain First World status. Thus in the noughties, the arts was rationalised for nation-branding. We had Singapore Season in cities like London, Moscow and Beijing. We also had Spotlight on Singapore in Hong Kong and other cities where Singapore wanted to improve its trade agreements. The arts served as a seat-warmer, paving the way for the business community and politicians.

These were the stages of arts development from the 1980s till today. KPIs (Key Performance Indicators), rationalised to achieve nation-building goals, helped secure sustained government funding for the arts. With that, the arts in Singapore enjoyed exponential growth. What has taken Singapore 25 years to develop would have taken another country about 60 years or more. Because of our size and top-down planned social change, Singapore grew from a cultural desert to a country with numerous arts and cultural activities on any one night. In other words, the state's continued emphasis on nation-building prompted the development of the arts in Singapore.

Very rarely is the arts supported for its inherent worth.

Present Imperfect

> Once there was this man who was invited to his girlfriend's house for Christmas dinner. During dinner, he noticed that the roast turkey's head and back were both chopped off. He was curious, so after the meal, he questioned his girlfriend. But, she too didn't know why. All her life the turkey had been served that way. So, they went to ask her mother. Her mother didn't know as well. Ever since she was a child, turkey was always served that way. So, finally, they went to ask the girl's grandmother, who was old and bedridden. Her grandmother said that when she was young, her family couldn't afford a big oven. So every time they wanted turkey, they

had to cut off its head and back so that it could fit into their oven. That was the reason why in that household the turkey will always be served with its head and back chopped off.[2]

In the 1980s and 1990s, censorship was under the direct purview of the police. All shows had to secure a Public Entertainment Licence before they could open. In 2003, this role was taken over by the Media Development Authority (MDA). MDA became the buffer between the artists and the police. MDA shifted the responsibilities of regulation away from the NAC by developing a rating and advisory system so that a range of works could be shown, enhancing the diversity in our cultural performance landscape. Yet somehow, the arts ecology continues to be shaped by these policies which testify to the government's idea of how the arts should look like in this nation-state.

On the other hand, the various theatre companies have continued to explore their respective ideas of nation in their works. For TNS, this has meant moving from multicultural theatre to intercultural theatre. Whilst multiculturalism to me is the acknowledgement of different cultures existing in one geographical space, interculturalism would refer to the interaction of different cultures, the latter being a more sophisticated concept, to politically re-imagine how we can work and live across differences. This is an important instrument for us Singaporeans as we are not Japan, China, India, Hong Kong or Indonesia. We are not anchored in one mother culture as we have different cultures co-existing here. We may have hybridised ethnic categories such as Eurasians and Peranakans (Straits-born Chinese). Unlike Japan where one is Japanese only by birth, a highly skilled foreigner can become a permanent resident and eventually become Singaporean. Our national identity is seen as pretty fluid, open to being constructed through marriage and so, interculturalism would be best suited for a country/nation that is a product of the global village era.

Multiculturalism is a failed concept. A country like France can be cosmopolitan but social integration is through assimilation and

---

[2]Sharma, Haresh, *This Chord and Others*. Singapore: The Necessary Stage.

not necessarily by a cross-pollination of local and foreign cultures. That would require an acceptance of an outside culture on an almost equal status with its original or local one. Singapore embraces the Chinese-inclined Peranakans, the Malay-inclined Peranakans, Indian Peranakans and a continuum of Eurasians, which goes to show that there is no one culture that dominates another but an interaction of two or more cultural sensibilities producing plural, constructed cultural or ethnic categories. So, although the official categories are C (Chinese), I (Indians), M (Malays) and O (Others), a number of intercultural hybrids co-exist in modern Singapore.

These intercultural relationships can easily flow into cultural productions in terms of language, costume, world views and sensibilities. Since there is no censorship in these areas, their representations are not suppressed and therefore can become subject matter and/or issues addressed in contemporary art works. Such diversity, if allowed to proliferate in the arts ecology, can then substantiate the term "Uniquely Singapore". But very quickly this is complicated with the inflow of new immigrants and new citizens in recent years. More cultural hybrids are now made possible, destabilising what has existed over the past decades. Having said that, whatever the case may be, Singapore is a nation, country and a space which spawns, welcomes and nurtures the interaction of diverse cultural identities. There will never be an end to producing cultural hybrids. We should revisit the historical identity of Singapore as the centre of entrepôt trade which was responsible for how we thrived in our early days. It has always been a meeting point, a strategic geographical position, a confluence for an exchange and trade in ideas and commodities.

Now, if only the richness of cross-pollination can benefit the nation more effectively. There is a sense that we are not capitalising on our intercultural strengths, our capacity and capabilities. Once they appear on the government's radar and make economic sense, there would be more research and development support. But for now, it is left to the artists to continue in their mission of engendering our nationhood. Our adventure to re-imagine what we are all about, as a people sharing a common geographical space living within the same political, economic, socio-cultural context responding daily to a global village which becomes increasingly more borderless each day. In the meantime, we have to be thinking out of the box — contemporise tradition, break away from tradition, re-imagine new guidelines that lead us to transit from just a local mindset to one that facilitates constant mobility between local and international contexts.

Sustainability

It is essential for a theatre company to be able to think out of the box and be realistic and pragmatic when it comes to forging ways to be sustainable whilst not falling too far behind living standards and/or not having the integrity of one's mission/vision compromised. A case in point is TNS' ability to secure external projects which, over the years, enabled us to remain in the black whilst pursuing our idealistic projects: 23% of TNS' operation cost is covered by a two-year grant by the NAC, subject to review. The other 77%, is what the company has to raise on its own. Thus, we created External Projects. This helps us secure commissioned projects which we do not publicise in the media so as to avoid branding confusion. At the same time, however, the company earns some money to make up for the loss we make staging our idealistic works.

All the pioneer theatre companies have developed their capacities with respect to the NAC subsidy funding and whatever other funds they are able to secure elsewhere — external projects, school and community outreach initiatives, philanthropists, fundraising, foundations, corporate sponsorship and marketing initiatives. As theatre became part of our landscape, with its education scaffolding developed over the years in our education system (drama programmes and modules inhabit the curriculum at schools, polytechnics, junior colleges and universities), more voluntary welfare and not-for-profit organisations starting to employ theatre to raise awareness of their respective missions, it became commonplace for these groups to start looking for help from theatre companies rather than the other way around, which was the case in the 1980s and early 1990s. This shift in the landscape created a vital and growing market, paving the way for more arts projects to be supported throughout the nation, thus providing jobs for more artists over the last decade. This made it possible for parents to not be as anxious as parents of the 1980s generation — they are more assured that their children would be able to find stable careers in the arts when they graduate. Those not academically-inclined also saw more hope in developing their non-academic talent and the market grew healthily and steadily in the late 1990s into the twenty-first century.

As the arts develop in Singapore, the dominant regulatory ethos has tended to be "Don't bite the hand that feeds you." Today, grants can be cut or an arts organisation can request that their logos not be used when a play is controversial. If a play is rated for adults and not for students, grants pertaining to their age group will not be made available to them. A theatre or arts venue is encouraged not to co-present works that are deemed controversial by MDA. Before making the cut in grants, the authorities employed cruder approaches which attracted a great deal of local and international media attention that also meant resources spent on public relations work to address perceptions after censoring a theatre event.

The authorities became more careful in minimising media attention and started corporatising and administering censorship so that it became more invisible. They penalise through grants, the use of logos and even through the use of arts housing or buildings belonging to the Government. For example, plays staged in buildings belonging to the Government must not run against core values or offend sensibilities. This is stated in the tenancy agreement for the arts housing scheme and has recently been highlighted, thus causing arts venues to be more cautious than before. In this way, the authorities continue to shape what kind of art should be encouraged and what kind of art, artists should stay away from.

Theatre companies that stage socially-engaged works continue to face obstacles. Drama Box, which creates forum theatre pieces that deal with controversial topics and play to communities at HDB estates, has faced challenges. MDA has requested, for example, that they cordon off their acting areas, create a stage under some kind of tentage (or marquee) and not play in open spaces.

Wild Rice has received funding cuts with their grants from the NAC due to the types of plays they have been staging. Yes, TNC has been allowed to stage plays that deal with child sexuality in a Muslim home (*Fundamentally Happy*), consumption of marijuana for palliative care and death penalty (*Good People*), political detention without trial (*Gemuk Girls*) and censorship (*Balek Kampong*) with just advisories. Perhaps it is because we discuss and negotiate our plans with MDA, perhaps it is because we play to small audiences (we are considered niche) in a small blackbox, so what we show is very contained and our runs are not long. If we are allowed to exist and our plays are allowed to be staged, socially-engaged works do see the light of day in Singapore so the authorities can use them as examples, especially to foreign investors, that Singapore is liberalising.

It is anyone's guess what the state's intent is but we remain grateful that we are able to keep our integrity intact with the idealistic works we wish to stage. In the long run, perhaps we are gradually creating an alternate reality in Singapore before its time and are sowing the seeds for a more progressive and open society. Every step matters. Every play we stage is a triumph no matter how small an audience we reach out to.

When a small space opens up, dance like mad.

JULIANA LIM (daughter of a Chinese father and Malay mother) IS GIVING A SPEECH IN MANDARIN, MALAY AND ENGLISH.

[Mandarin]

My fellow Singaporeans. At today's National Day Speech,

I am happy to declare that Singapore is progressing…and progressive!

We are a global powerhouse. Singapore of the past was built on solid foundations.

We weathered troubled times and sailed through with a strong economy.

Despite one financial crisis after another, our economy never weakened.

[Malay]

Since I have become Prime Minister, I have also focused on other issues — issues which had not been such a priority in the past.

Several Bills have been passed in recent months. Now our Migrant Workers — or Guest Workers as they're called now — enjoy the same rights as all foreign employees. The elderly, the poor and the underprivileged have free medical benefits.

We have spent too much time and resource on the hardware.

Now is a time to spare a thought for our heart-ware.

[English]

There is also greater individual freedom and right to expression.

I am therefore proud to announce that the first Singapore Peace and Freedom Award will be presented, posthumously, to my grandfather... Marzuki Bin Abdul Rahman.

Marzuki Bin Abdul Rahman was detained in 1962. He was suspected of being involved in the communist faction and his failure to confess resulted in longer-term detention. He was never charged in court, and was never reunited with his family. Today is a day of change. Today we celebrate him, honour him. Today, as PM, I urge you, my fellow Singaporeans, to honour him.

This award signals a new era. No longer do we have to live in fear. No longer do we have to silence our thoughts, or censor our views. No longer do we need to stifle our voices. And I am happy to say that despite your new-found freedom, there has been no voice of discontent. No protests. No riots. No petitions. No letters of complaints. There is no opposition.

Today, on her 63rd birthday, this country has come of age. We are a force to be reckoned with. Today, on her 63rd birthday, Singapore has finally gained true independence. We can be proud to say, 'I am a Singaporean. I am a Singaporean'.

[pause]

LET US ALL STAND FOR OUR NATIONAL ANTHEM.[3]

[3] Sharma, Haresh, *Gemuk Girls.* Singapore: The Necessary Stage.

Chapter 4

The Singapore Story: The Writing and Rewriting of a History*

Kwa Chong Guan

*This article was originally published in Commentary, Volume 22 titled "The Idea of Singapore" © 2013 The National University of Singapore Society. Kwa Chong Guan is Senior Fellow at S. Rajaratnam School of International Studies, Nanyang Technological University, Singapore.

In 1987, Mr S Rajaratnam, then Senior Minister in the Prime Minister's Office, confidently declared that "until very recently, Singapore's past was a matter of supreme indifference for most Singaporeans because they believed this island never really had a history worth remembering." As Rajaratnam pointed out, "our history began in 1819 when Raffles landed in swampy Singapore with some 40 to 50 unremarkable kampong houses and no more than 400 Malays, Orang Laut and a sprinkling of very lost Chinese. This is not the stuff which enthralling history is made out of. Nothing very much appears to have happened in Singapore — if anything happened at all — before Raffles landed in this unpromising island." The argument Rajaratnam was leading up to, was that "though our history began in 1819, this brief past is what made Singapore and its people what they are today, and it is this Singapore's past which will shape their future and furnish the ingredients for a national identity."[1]

On hindsight, Rajaratnam has played a lead role in reconstructing Singapore's past to "shape its future and furnish the ingredients for a national identity." In a little-known and under-appreciated 1965 reflection on the PAP's First Ten Years in Power, Rajaratnam outlined the kernel of what has become the Singapore Story.

Rajaratnam assured People's Action Party (PAP) members that the Party had much to be proud of on its 10th anniversary. Writing in the midst of a political crisis in relations with Kuala Lumpur, Rajaratnam could still confidently declare that the Party had "achieved one of its fundamental aims: The independence of Singapore through merger with the Federation of Malaya." In an oblique reference to the ongoing political crisis the Party was embroiled in, Rajaratnam claimed that the PAP had been able to "thwart the manoeuvres of both the right-wing reactionaries and the communist on the far left with a fair degree of success."[2]

---

[1] Rajaratnam's speech at an old National Museum Gallery exhibition, reprinted in Kwa, Chong Guan (ed.), *S Rajaratnam on Singapore: From Ideas to Reality* (Singapore: World Scientific Publishing & Institute of Defence & Strategic Studies, 2006), 264.

[2] PAP's First Ten Years in Power, reprinted in *Rajaratnam on Singapore*, 180–226.

Rajaratnam recounted the founding of the Party in the basement dining room of Lee Kuan Yew's Oxley Road residence and what prompted a group of political neophytes to establish a new left-wing party against better-established political parties in an increasingly divided political arena. The bulk of reflections outlined the dilemmas and choices the Party faced as it decided how to achieve its agenda without being co-opted by other right-wing parties or subverted by the Communist. In terms of genres of stories, Rajaratnam's story of the PAP has all the elements of a heroic romance, like Edmund Spenser's narrative of the quest of St George in *The Faerie Queene*, of a perilous journey undertaken in fulfilment of a quest for a grail, or in this case, a vision of a democratic socialist society. This journey culminates in an epic struggle with the Communist in which either the hero, his foe, or both, must die. In this case, fortunately the hero was victorious in the 1963 elections.

However, this heroic struggle against colonialism, communism and communalism for Singapore's place in a "Malaysian Malaysia" ended in the tragedy of Separation. Whereas the PAP leaders may have put behind them the trauma of 9 August 1965 as a foundational historical event, the experience of that tragedy continued to haunt them and their vision for Singapore, like Hamlet haunted and driven by his father's ghost to a tragic conclusion. The PAP leaders acted to exorcise the ghost of Separation by disproving the deeply-held historical assumption that Singapore, divorced from its peninsula hinterland, would collapse and prove instead that Singapore as a city-state could survive the odds.

By 1973, Singapore's dependence upon its traditional port functions of financing, processing, marketing and exporting the staple products of the Malay Peninsula and the archipelago had been broken. Export of Singapore's manufactures and expansion of financial and other business services underpinned a growing Singapore economy. Rajaratnam could confidently explain to the Singapore Press Club in 1972 why Singapore was proving wrong its critics and other pessimists who believed that separated from its peninsula hinterland, Singapore would collapse. The country, according to Rajaratnam, was transforming itself from a "trading city of Southeast Asia, the market place of the region...into a new kind of city — the Global City."[3] In making this claim, Rajaratnam was prescient, for the end of the Cold War which would enable a new cycle of globalisation and the emergence of a new global economy networked around a number of world cities, was twenty years in the future.

By the early 1980s, Singapore was taxiing down the runway for an economic takeoff. Rajaratnam and his colleagues could again reflect and reconfigure their memories of why Singapore had not failed. In their recollections, the odds were stacked against it and Singapore should have failed. Declaring the opening of an $18 million "National Exhibition" to celebrate 25 years of Independence in 1984, then Prime Minister Lee Kuan Yew rhetorically asked, "We survived. Later, we prospered. How did it happen? The basic attributes of nationhood were missing. We were groups of diverse and different peoples. We had no common past. We had no common language, culture or religion. We did not have 'the social glue' to hold together as a nation." This "National Exhibition" and a series of other exhibitions at the old National Museum and the National Archives over the next decade crafted this story of how Singapore survived and developed against the odds.

However, contained in this story of survival and development were the seeds of its unravelling. For as Singapore developed, it also forgot its past. Urban redevelopment removed landmarks that were sites of memories and history. New memories of redeveloped sites such as Raffles Place or Orchard Road had little, if any, connection with memories of the old Raffles Place or Orchard Road. The Housing and Development Board (HDB) estates developed in the 1970s and 1980s are unmemorable compared to the old *kampongs*. A new ordering of our work, social and family lives reconfigured the old social memories we inherited. The politically tumultuous and economically uncertain past could be forgotten in the prosperous and stable present. A post-1965 generation of Singaporeans grew up

[3] Singapore: Global City, reprinted in *Rajaratnam on Singapore*, 227–237.

learning to forget the past of their parents as new social memories were created.

In 1996, then Prime Minister Goh Chok Tong raised the alarm when he realised that "younger Singaporeans knew very little of the events and issues surrounding our independence." Goh pointed out that "not knowing the circumstances of Singapore's birth is a serious gap in knowledge...of how we became a nation, and the principles of meritocracy and multiracialism which underpin our entire society and political culture." To rectify this, Goh proposed a National Education Programme to "engender a shared sense of nationhood, an understanding of how our past is relevant to our present and future. It must appeal to both heart and mind." The National Education Programme which was launched the following year by then Deputy Prime Minister Lee Hsien Loong, has today become a major component of a more holistic national education curriculum with the Singapore Story as its bedrock.[4]

The Singapore Story of how it succeeded against the odds to become a nation took definite shape in a multimillion dollar exhibition launched in July 1998. *The Singapore Story: Overcoming the Odds* guided its visitors in a people-mover system around a series of tableaux depicting Singapore's historical development from the hardship of the Japanese Occupation through the post-World War II anti-colonial struggle for independence, and fight against Communism to negotiations to form Malaysia. How Singapore responded to the dire political and economic challenges confronting the nascent city-state after Separation from the Federation is depicted in the concluding section of this exhibition. This story has been recounted in detail and finesse by Lee Kuan Yew in his two-volume *memoire.*

The story was further consolidated in an audio-visual documentary proposed by then Prime Minister Goh to honour Lee Kuan Yew on his 80th birthday in 2003. Two years in the making, the

---

[4]Ministry of Education (MOE) National Education (NE), PM Goh and DPM Lee on National Education, Ministry of Education (MOE) & National Education (NE), retrieved from www.ne.edu.sg [speeches]. Also note additional NE information retrieved from Ministry of Defence (MINDEF), www.nexus.gov.sg.

three-hour multimillion dollar documentary produced by Discovery Channel Asia was broadcast on 4 and 5 December 2005 as a commemoration of Singapore's 40th anniversary. The underlying theme of this documentary was that Singapore's transformation from *Mangrove to Metropolis,* as the documentary was entitled, was in large part driven by the vision of a series of "Great Men" from Sir Stamford Raffles to Lee Kuan Yew.

The Singapore Story, as one structured around heroes and villains, attributes to the PAP leaders the vision, leadership and gumption to lead Singapore through its anti-colonial struggle to Independence in a merger to form Malaysia and then through the trauma of Separation to survive and prosper. This rationale for making the story of the PAP the plot of The Singapore Story was articulated by Rajaratnam in his address at a 1984 Pre-University Seminar. Rajaratnam provocatively asked his audience, "If not the Singapore created by the PAP, then what kind of Singapore would have emerged in its place?" Rajaratnam's response to his counterfactual question was to paint to his audience in his usual purple prose, the dark hues of a communist Singapore.[5] *Men in White* by Sonny Yap, Richard Lim and Leong Weng Kam reworks in detail this articulation of the PAP with Singapore's history.

As a genre of writing about the past in terms of the "Great Men" who made history, The Singapore Story is not unusual, but it does raise a number of issues. The first issue is that it evokes a response from those vanquished or castigated as communist to argue for their version of the past. Poh Soo Kai, Tan Jing Quee and Koh Kay Yew have invited some of their fellow political activists to join them in reflecting on their place in history.[6] Poh's reflections on his detention in Operation Cold Store in 1963 offers an alternative reconstruction of the event to that in The Singapore Story. Tan Jing Quee has also collaborated with Tan Kok Chiang and Hong Lysa to

[5] Birth of a Nation, *Rajaratnam on Singapore,* 263.

[6] Poh, Soo Kai, Tan, Jing Quee, and Koh, Kay Yew (eds.), *The Fajar Generation: The University Socialist Club and the Politics of Postwar Malaya and Singapore* (Petaling Jaya: Strategic Information and Research Development Centre, 2010).

offer an alternative interpretation of Chinese school activism as a struggle over issues of their identity as Chinese/Malayan/ Singaporean.[7] Others, like Fong Chong Pik, whom some of us recognise as the "Plen" Lee Kuan Yew met, has written his memoirs,[8] as has Said Zahari.[9] Lim Chin Siong has been remembered by his comrades in a series of tributes as a *Comet in Our Sky*.[10]

The second issue is the critical examination of the historiography of this Singapore Story by a younger generation of historians. Hong Lysa and Huang Jianli lead in their critique of *The Scripting of a National History*.[11] *Paths Not Taken: Political Pluralism in Post-War Singapore* edited by Michel D Barr and Carl Trocki[12] brings together a wider range of Singaporean and other scholars to examine the possibilities of history which the 1950s and 1960s offered. Loh Kah Seng and Liew Kai Khiun have brought together a group of younger historians to discuss the issues and difficulties they encountered in attempting to get past *The Makers & Keepers of Singapore History* to reconstruct other multiple understandings of our past with The Singapore Story as but one such understanding.[13] A number of blogs and online journals such as *s/pores*, have emerged to join this examination of the writing of Singapore history.

---

[7] Tan, Jing Quee, Tan, Kok Chiang, and Hong, Lysa (eds.), *The May 13 Generation; The Chinese Middle Schools Student Movement and Singapore Politics in the 1950s* (Petaling Jaya: Strategic Information and Research Development Centre, 2011).

[8] Fong, Chong Pik, *The Memoirs of a Malayan Communist Revolutionary* (Petaling Jaya: Strategic Information and Research Development Centre, 2008).

[9] Zahari, Said, *The Long Nightmare: My 17 Years as a Political Prisoner* (Kuala Lumpur: Utusan Publications, 2007).

[10] Tan, Jing, Quee, and Jomo, K S (eds.), *Comet in Our Sky: Lim Chin Siong in History* (Kuala Lumpur: INSAN, 2001).

[11] Hong, Lysa, and Huang, Jianli, *The Scripting of a National History: Singapore and Its Pasts* (Singapore: NUS Press, 2008).

[12] Barr, Michael, and Trocki, Carl A. (eds.), *Paths Not Taken: Political Pluralism in Post-war Singapore* (Singapore: NUS Press, 2008).

[13] Loh, Kah Seng, and Liew, Kai Khiun (eds.), *The Makers & Keepers of Singapore History* (Singapore: Ethos Books/Singapore Heritage Society, 2010).

Complementing this examination of the historiography of The Singapore Story is the attempt to reframe it in a wider spatial context and longer temporal span. Derek Heng has been developing this approach to Singapore's past.[14] He had earlier joined Tan Tai Yong and the author of this essay to argue that Singapore has a 700-year history.[15] This reconstruction of a 700-year history for Singapore is based in large part on the archaeological excavations undertaken by John Miksic since 1984 and the pioneering work of Peter Borschberg on the 17th century Portuguese-Dutch rivalry for control of the waters of Singapore and Melaka Straits.[16]

A third set of issues that The Singapore Story evokes is the experience and social memories of living out the narrative of it. Like the pioneering generation of poets, dramatists and artists who captured their experiences of living through the anti-colonial struggle of the 1950s and 1960s in their works, a post-1965 generation of the same are recording their experiences of living The Singapore Story too. For example, Alfian Saat agonises about his identity in multiethnic and multicultural Singapore in his poetry. Tan Pin Pin deploys her cinematic skills to document the trauma of relocating from an old *kampong* to a modern HDB flat or the spatial justice of exhuming an old cemetery.

---

[14] Heng, Derek Thiam Soon (ed.), *New Perspectives and Sources on the History of Singapore: A Multi-Disciplinary Approach* (Singapore: National Library Board, 2006); Heng, Derek Thiam Soon, and Aljunied, Syed Muhd Khairudin (eds.), *Reframing Singapore: Memory-Identity-Trans-Regionalism* (Amsterdam: Amsterdam University Press/ICAS Publ.6, 2006); Heng, Derek Thiam Soon, and Aljunied, Syed Muhd Khairudin (eds.), *Singapore in Global History* (Amsterdam: Amsterdam University Press/ICAS Publ.14, 2011).

[15] Kwa, Chong Guan, Heng, Derek Thiam Soon, and Tan, Tai Yong, *Singapore: A 700-Year History: From Early Emporium to World City* (Singapore: National Archives of Singapore, 2009).

[16] Miksic, John N., and Low, Cheryl-Ann Mei Gek (eds.), *Early Singapore, 1300s–1819: Evidence in Maps, Text and Artefacts* (Singapore: Singapore History Museum, 2004); Borschberg, Peter, *The Singapore and Melaka Straits; Violence, Security and Diplomacy in the 17th Century* (Singapore: NUS Press, 2010).

The Singapore Story has become an integral component of Singapore's identity today. As such, this essay argues, the Singapore Story is contemporary history which the Italian historian and philosopher Benedetto Croce defined the "living history" of those who had a part in the making of that history or were a witness to it. It is a justification of that immediate past for the present and a projection of that lessons and prospects for the future. Narrating the end of the Cold War raises issues of the triumphalism of Democracy and the "End of History" as Francis Fukuyama once expressed it. This raises issues of the visions of social and spatial justice embedded in any narrative of contemporary history. Visions of a meritocratic, multiethnic and multicultural society underpin the Singapore Story and raises issues of the translation of those visions into government policies and plans. The controversy over the preservation of the cemetery on Bukit Brown or earlier, the redevelopment of Chinatown, or quotas of foreign labour are contestations over the policy implications of progress and equality embedded in The Singapore Story of Singapore's transformation from a colonial port city to a city-state and into a global city today.

Chapter 5

Imagining Singapore 2030: Language, Demographics and the Region*

Yang Razali Kassim

*This article was originally published in Commentary, Volume 22 titled "The Idea of Singapore" © 2013 The National University of Singapore Society. The late Yang Razali Kassim was a Senior Fellow at S. Rajaratnam School of International Studies, Nanyang Technological University, Singapore. He had been Chairman of the Association of Muslim Professionals and was a career journalist.

Preamble: Vision 2030

As Singaporeans embark on a rare moment of introspection and ponder their future in a national exercise called "Our Singapore Conversation", one question must not be forgotten: What will we look like to the outside world, especially the immediate region, by 2030? To put it in another way: What kind of Singapore will we be from our neighbours' perspectives, three decades from now? Will we become even more enmeshed with our surroundings? Or will we, on the contrary, become more different, more distant and more detached and aloof from our neighbours? Whichever way it turns out, will the future face of Singapore strengthen or compromise the Republic's position as a nation-state by 2030?

These are fundamental questions. In fact, they are as fundamental as the ones that modern Singapore's founding fathers grappled with since Independence in 1965. The answers will depend very much on how Singapore society will have evolved three decades hence. Needless to say, so much already has changed over the last six decades since Singapore was thrust into existence as an independent state in a region that was ambivalent to, if not unsure of, its arrival. Yet, there are clear constants that have defined, and will continue to define Singapore as it moves forward. The primary and overriding constant is its survival as a nation-state, the key determinants of which are political stability and economic viability, both in turn dependent on the cohesion of the various communities.

Arising from these constants, government leaders proclaim without fail the three unchanging principles of governance — multiracialism, multiculturalism and meritocracy — which guide the Singaporean nation-state through the choppy waters of time as a polyglot nation. These three principles have shaped the process of nation-building as the founding leaders of Singapore walked a tightrope between forging a multiethnic, multireligious and multicultural nation and pursuing their early politics of identity, at the heart of which were language and culture.

Generational Change and Continuity

The evolution of Singaporean society has gone through two generations — the Lee Kuan Yew era and the Goh Chok Tong era — and is now being steered through the third, the Lee Hsien Loong era. Prime Minister (PM) Lee recently signalled that he does not expect to still be in office at the age of 70. In other words, well before 2030, there will be a new prime minister. When PM Lee hands over to his successor, the transition will be just as equally shaped by the forces of change and continuity: Like his two predecessors, PM Lee will be stepping down in his 60s but unlike them, he will be handing over to a leader who, for the first time, will come from the post-Independence generation.

But what will the Lee Hsien Loong era leave behind and what kind of nation will the next PM take over? How similar or how different will the fourth PM be from his predecessors? Will he stick to the principles of governance and leadership that have guided Singapore since Independence? How will the new leader balance the imperative of leading Singaporeans into the uncharted future while not forgetting the past so that the Singapore of 2030 is not something totally strange?

Language, Politics and the Region

There will be many challenges, of course, as the future PM straddles between change and continuity. However, one of the unbending core issues three decades from now will be the role of language in nation-building, in a country that will be increasingly diverse due to immigration. In this respect, there is one convention that has always been upheld but seldom talked about and yet, is actually significant. At the National Day Rally (NDR) in August 2012, PM Lee spoke in three languages — Malay, Mandarin and English — in that order. They were not mere translations of the same speech but messages tailored specifically to the different audiences and constituencies. This sequence of speeches has been customary since the first NDR after Independence in 1965. Presumably, the rationale is to signify Malay as the national language, Mandarin as the language of the majority ethnic group in Singapore and English as the working language of all Singaporeans. Together with Tamil, these make up the four official languages. Indeed, upholding the same language policy can also be observed at the annual conferences of the ruling People's Action Party (PAP), where the Party's Secretary-General, who is the PM, similarly speaks in the three languages, and in that order.

Why does the PM still speak in Malay first instead of English or Mandarin? It is a political statement, no doubt. PM Lee is continuing a conscious policy that, at first glance, is more symbolic than substantive. Like his two predecessors, Mr Lee Kuan Yew and Mr Goh Chok Tong, PM Lee is upholding the national language — something he has been doing without fail at every NDR since he became PM in 2004. Yet, if we think more deeply about it, we will realise that the symbolism is loaded with subtle signals about what we are as a nation.

Whenever the PM speaks in Malay — and Malay first — it is no exaggeration to say that it evokes a certain emotion — for Singaporeans as a whole because their PM has that rare mastery of languages to connect with the people; for the Malays in Singapore, whom the Constitution recognises as the indigenous people because the PM speaks their language; and for the political leadership because the PM is able to send a powerful, though unstated message about the genesis, history and uniqueness of Singapore as a nation-state. In an age of instant and global communication, it is a message that is invariably heard around the region and increasingly at the people level as well. For instance, in a blog posted in the *EC Malaysian Blog* entitled "PM Lee's Malay Speech at National Day Rally 2012", blogger ECGMA writes: "PM Lee Hsien Loong speaks the Malay language impressively, better than many of us in Malaysia, including local politicians and me!".

Beyond the symbolism, the subtext between the lines each time the PM delivers his annual direction-setting address in Malay, followed by Mandarin and English, comes in layered meanings for two different audiences. For Singaporeans, the first and probably the most significant is that despite four decades of Independence, Singapore does not forget its roots. It may be a legacy of Singapore's early political history forged by the battle for merger with Malaysia that Malay remains the national language. But it is a legacy that also has its utility as a unifier of a multicultural nation. Thus the national anthem is still in Malay and uniformed groups — the military, police and civil defence — go by drill commands in Malay. While it is true that all these are largely perfunctory, they remain a key shaper for the consciousness of Singaporeans of where they belong in their collective memory as one people in spite of their diverse origins. Equally important is the message to the outside world that Singapore sees itself as being very much a part of Southeast Asia — despite being an independent and highly globalised nation-state which is majority ethnic Chinese, it is located in a Malay sea. There is an unstated reason for this display of tolerance and mutual accommodation — to be the living antithesis of whoever is not tolerant or accommodating.

There is yet another rationale, best captured in the words of Singapore's first Prime Minister. On 3 October 1965, two months after separating from Malaysia, the man who was responsible for the national language policy, then PM Lee Kuan Yew, said, "Why have we to accept Malay as our National Language? For on principle, that is correct. Why must we have four languages, and at the same time let them have equal positions? The reason is, this is good for our country. We can become a model, not only for the whole of Southeast Asia to see, but also for the Afro-Asian countries to see." A year later, at the opening of a Tamil school on 19 December 1966, Mr Lee expanded on this, spelling out the need to give space to each community to have its language, culture and identity, "But to each also must be given the maximum of common denominators without which you and I will never be able to understand each other…And so it is that we have designated that Malay should be our National Language."

In other words, the Malay language was meant to be the bridge linking the various communities even as all the main languages are given equal status. By making Malay his first language of delivery at every NDR, the current PM signals that this policy remains valid. The message for Singaporeans is this: Even as the little red dot continues to differentiate itself from the region as a strategy for survival, using Malay as the national language is a core policy as provided for in the Constitution. It is an important signal that while Singapore will be increasingly different as it evolves into a future entity, it will still be anchored to the region and its past in terms of its identity as a nation-state. It is a fine balancing act whose deep significance will only be appreciated when lost.

So, will the future PM in 2030 be able to perpetuate this policy? More importantly, will the next PM want this policy to continue to hold? Will he have the facility with the language to help him sustain it and communicate his vision, policies and ethos, bearing in mind that he will be a product of post-Separation Singapore in which Malay as the national language is more symbolic than functional? How will the Government uphold this constitutional imperative in the face of the demographic trends currently sweeping Singapore which will have significant bearing on the future?

Impact of Changing Demographics

On 29 January 2013, the Government stunned Singaporeans with a White Paper that projected a population growth of up to 6.9 million by 2030, from the current 5.3 million. Describing 2012 as a turning point in the trend towards an ageing society, it was likely that almost half the projected population would comprise foreigners as the Government pursues a policy of active though moderated immigration to offset the demographic trends. After intense debate in Parliament and amidst an anxious populace, the Government adopted the White Paper. The anxieties of Singaporeans over the impact and implications of the demographic trends however, remain strong at the people level, having surfaced as a major political issue in the general election of 2011. National leaders stress that immigration is critical to the survival of Singapore in the long term. Yet, as with most countries receiving immigration, this trend is causing restiveness and a sense of disempowerment. However, the fear of further political backlash on the PAP government has led to the pace of immigration being tempered, even as the broader policy of remaining open to immigration is sustained. At the same time, we are beginning to feel the palpable sense of unease and dislocation leading to Singaporean society coming closer together. "core Singaporeans" — those born and bred in Singapore — are seeking comfort in each other as they adjust to what they feel as unsettling change. In the process, we are noticing a heightened sense of common identity among the core Singaporeans. PM Lee spoke of how we are beginning to see Singaporean-Chinese being different from China-Chinese, Singaporean-Indians being different from India-Indians, and possibly Singaporean-Malays too from other Southeast Asian-Malays. In the cyberworld, we see the Singaporean identity being reinforced by the unpleasant side effects of immigration, and people developing closer bonds amongst themselves as core Singaporeans.

The best example of this is the Amy Cheong controversy which saw non-Malay Singaporeans coming to the defence of Malay Singaporeans in the face of what was described as the racist rantings of the Malaysia-born Australian Ms Cheong who was unhappy with the noise from Malay weddings held in Housing and Development Board (HDB) void decks. Even PM Lee had to come down on her. If the Amy Cheong saga is any indicator of the future, the core Singaporeans from the different communities will increasingly huddle together and seek comfort in their common bonds in the face of discomforting change. Notice how Singaporeans of diferent races became uneasy with Singapore Mass Rapid Transit's (SMRT) attempt to translate the names of local train stations from English into Mandarin only, ostensibly to make it easier for tourists from China to navigate their way around. The growing clamour for more sensitivity towards the feelings of the locals forced SMRT to drop the project.

Going Forward

In the years to come, as the pressures of demographic change increase and as Singaporeans clutch what can bind them even more closely as well as anchor them for a sense of stability, they will see the value of the bridges that forge their common Singaporean identity. Such bonds will take many forms. These will inevitably include the languages that they have grown up with and been moulded by — be they English, Mandarin, Tamil, Malay or even *Singlish.* It is under such future circumstances that the role of the national language may prove its utility as the glue that it was always meant to be. Will the national language still be upheld then or will the tide of immigration lead to its further erosion or neglect? Should we allow this to happen?

Indeed, will English remain the working language in Singapore as the rise of China leads to its economic preponderance? Will immigration over time lead to the emergence of a generation of "new Singaporeans" who do not have a strong appreciation or attachment, if at all, to the history that made Singapore unique, such that a minority language can become the national language? Will there be the political will on the part of future leaders to retain Malay as the national language that binds the multiracial and multicultural nation?

As we ponder our future, we may have to consider the fundamental forces that keep the idea of a Singaporean Singapore alive — and the uniqueness that makes the country what it is today. There may well be a need to "revive" the national language beyond its current symbolic role precisely because of the need to bind anew everyone — including the new citizens — to the idea of a Singaporean Singapore. In schools where future generations are shaped, our children, be they the offsprings of core or new Singaporeans, will need to be exposed in a more purposeful way to the importance of all the major languages — including the national language. As one Singaporean Chinese blogger, *gintai,* says in his post entitled "Malay is still the National Language of Singapore": "I feel that if Malay is accorded the National Language status, then it should be treated as such. Not only our National Anthem is sung in Malay on National Day or on other official occasions, it is also the language of command in the armed forces. It should be much more than that."

As Asia rises further by 2030 driven by new economic powers such as China, India and possibly Indonesia, the Government's long-standing language policy of giving equal treatment to the four languages while making Malay the national language will increasingly prove far-sighted. In recent years, students have been allowed to take up third languages for their economic value. In the future, as Singapore plugs further into the globalised world and language options widen, there may be a need to strengthen the anchoring and stabilising role of the national language. While Chinese, Indian and students of other races should feel free to take up Malay as the national language, Malay students should fortify their mother tongue. They should not feel inhibited to take up Mandarin or even Indian languages as a third language so that they can benefit from the rising influence of the new economic powers. In this way, the Singapore of the 21st century will rise with Asia and yet remain the cohesive nation-state that it is meant to be.

Chapter 6

How Singapore can Transform Itself into a Creative Centre in the Region*

Tay Kheng Soon

*This article was originally published in Commentary, Volume 22 titled "The Idea of Singapore" © 2013 The National University of Singapore Society. Tay Kheng Soon, a practising architect since 1965, was an Adjunct Associate Professor at the Department of Architecture, School of Design and Environment, National University of Singapore.

Everything that happens in the world affects Singapore. When the big powers sneeze, we get a cold. Singapore is a third-world orphan that refused to be put down so its only way was up and so succeeded under the umbrella of its Western stepparents. However, Singapore's will to succeed was based on its own vision and discipline. But that discipline had a cost. The cost was the decline in authentic identity, lack of self-confidence and low levels of creativity. Initial creativity gave way to reliance on the best of others but not itself. While success brought pride, that pride was brittle. Together, these put the brakes on stepping out of the box.

This piece of fiction is about imagining how Singapore might find the courage to be creative all over again. This time, it is not the '60s sort of dire necessity that drives it but necessity of a different kind; it is an internal necessity to survive by becoming herself in a much changed world. How does this need arise in our fictional vision of Singapore in 2022? Usually at mid-life, people think again. Singapore is experiencing its own mid-life crisis. A crisis is always both a challenge and an opportunity. How Singapore will remake itself is the challenge. How it builds on its strengths is an opportunity and some things in the world can be bought cheap.

As I write this piece, I imagine it backwards from the vantage point of 2022 — how the new imperatives to transform ourselves come about. Strangely, it begins in the heart and in the heartlands. The need to re-integrate head, heart and hand was long awaited... life felt incomplete in the fragmented state...

The spark came about by a mindset change among a disenchanted bunch of bright young civil servants and their counterparts outside the public service. Returned scholars who had breathed a freer sort of air felt the atmosphere stifling. So they fretted, fearful at first to challenge the established views but by degrees, raised innocent but probing questions with prickly humour. This set off a chain of actions and reactions that led to rapped knuckles and red faces. It would have been left there but the rediscovery of lost threads in their own history and culture expunged from their consciousness brought an added sense of purpose and self-identity. They felt shortchanged in life after that.

Singapore's illiberal democracy had succeeded but it raised a feckless people and this disturbed members of this new thinking elite to no end. The stage was set for change…

Imagining Singapore in 2022

After the 2016 General Elections (GE), the ruling party saw more losses despite having courted the electorate for the past five years. The People's Action Party (PAP) had lost a Group Representation Constituency (GRC) in the 2011 GE; this time they lost several Single Member Constituencies. It was a new phenomenon indeed. Several independent candidates emerged victorious. It was a signal of the change in the polity; a rise of conscience politics; no ideology, no party, just individuals wanting change.

Something fundamental had happened in Singapore. Singaporeans wanted more heart and less dread. This GE led to another crisis in government. Government and Party were, till then, seen as one and the same but now, both split internally and between them; top civil servants were openly challenged by younger members. News filtered out from behind closed doors. The ultra-conservative Cabinet ministers were also challenged by ambitious young leaders. The time, it seemed, had come for the new in both the civil service and the Party.

The New Singapore Plan

After the 2016 GE, a new-look civil service eager to implement fresh ideas adopted a plan which had gathered dust since 2013 on how to turn Singapore smart at the grassroots level while accommodating a large influx of foreigners without stressing out the existing living environment of Singapore. The proposal was for a large area on the South Coast of the island stretching from Pandan Reservoir which included the National University of Singapore (NUS) all the way to East Coast Parkway to house at least a million people and became the high-tech creative centre of new Singapore. The development of this 23-kilometre belt began in 2017 and progressively became the workplace, waterfront residential zone and playground of the super smart and super creative. This became the creative heart of Singapore and it attracted among Singaporeans and the brightest and the best everywhere else to work, live, learn, play, farm and heal, and it became the cradle and incubator of Asia's new ideas, new products and new enterprises. All came, enticed by the sheer vibrancy of it.

New Planning Methodology

These urban planning ideas came about because of a new methodology called "3D Planning". The mismatch between new ideas and old planning methods was finally resolved. The old method was based on the matching of demographics to land use. These projections were based on existing building and occupancy typologies and building norms. Based on these, infrastructure, roads, water and electricity were allocated. This methodology was taught in all planning schools in the West and applied everywhere. They were premised on large land masses but were not appropriate for small places like Singapore. This led to mistaken notions of land shortage as there was a great deal of slippage in the floor area outcomes. Inherent errors occurred because floor space ratios were not computed island-wide and re-allocated appropriately.

Innovation in building design accelerated thereafter. The stagnation in design ended. The architectural profession had a lot of new thinking to do. Stacking, weaving, clustering, mixing and so on led to novel ways of optimising land usage while being consistent with livability and synergetic criteria. Accordingly, this methodology opened up many new possibilities in social design, physical planning and innovative architectural design beyond style.

Maintaining Social Cohesion

At such a rate of change in Singapore, there were two widening gaps — the income gap and the knowledge gap. Both threatened social cohesion. Without trust, the much-needed disruptive changes would be held back by negative social sentiment.

Addressing the Income Gap

While voluntary reductions of ministers' pay made an impression, it was the raising of minimum wage at the lowest wage level that helped mollify the negative sentiment. A whole slew of cost-cutting measures after the 2016 GE became necessary and a more equitable situation was created for a while. New values needed to be fostered. Democratising the social space, meaningful work, better family and community life, more involved participation, enlightenment, identity, better education — all these required a different approach than the carrot and stick method. Incentivisation which is external had to shift to internal motivation. The Maslowian hierarchy had changed with the advent of the information culture. As people know more, they demand dignity and self-actualisation at every stage of the ladder of needs they climb. The Government is compelled to match up to this new situation.

Addressing the Knowledge Gap

The digital divide was overcome but the vision gap was more difficult to tackle. If nothing was done to address this gap, there would be trouble. This gap was in the heartlands — the Housing and Development Board (HDB) estates. While education had always been a priority, thanks to the schools, the expansion of the polytechnics and the Institute of Technical Education (ITE), the establishment of many more universities and trans-location of many foreign branch campuses to Singapore, raised the general knowledge of ordinary Singaporeans. This was an urgent task but few knew how to do it. Some new ideas were thrown up in the "National Conversations" in 2012.

Inserting Smart Webs into HDB Estates

There was only so much that management, education and incentives could do. A change in the hearts and minds of the masses had to happen. The problem was how? This is where the idea of Smart Webs got dusted off and implemented.

Density there was, but what was missing was synergy. The Smart Webs did the trick. There was first the need to shift from the prevailing mechanistic way of seeing things, to the more complex biological way. Richard Florida's call for bohemian culture which only resulted in bartop dancing being allowed, had to go much further.

Inserting a Central Nervous System (CNS) into HDB Estates

In the biological imagination, a housing estate began to be thought of as a living organism and not as an efficient mechanism only. As such, the planners, architects and policy makers realised that what was needed was to emulate how high-functioning organisms work. The human system was the most complex. Realising this, the planners, architects and policy makers, backed by the community, began to plan and implement the linking of all the commercial, educational, artistic, financial, sports and civil-society facilities into one large network. The effect was electricfying! As this took place over the past 10 years, a new lease of life burst forth and a vibrant creativity became evident. The hitherto placid and *kiasu* mentality gave way to more expressive and entrepreneurial behaviour.

People, as they went about their daily routines, found themselves enjoying the liveliness of the Smart Webs. They naturally imbibed this through chance encounters with neighbours and new friends with new ideas. This was what high signal density and high signal diversity as found in high-functioning organisms and successful cities meant. These were the natural results derived from having a well-endowed nervous system: Sidewalk cafes, street art, school students, parents, teachers, office workers, artists, designers, research labs, prototyping workshops, performance theatres, adult education studios and the like mixed in with coffee shops, street stalls, groceries, restaurants and so on. The interaction between retail commerce, social clubs, civic activities, educational provision, humanitarian institutions and galleries all combined to produce a wonderful experience, everyday, for everyone.

Bukit Brown and the Rise of an Authentic Singaporean Identity

The popular movement to save the Bukit Brown Cemetery turned up many stories of long gone social heroes; heroes who made a difference in helping their fellow man. Sentimentality and nostalgia turned into self-discovery and thus authentic identity. As the stories of the lives and deeds of long ago Singaporean heroes circulated through the social media, a new self-appreciation began to form. These raised the level of self-respect and an authentic self-confidence among Singaporeans which laid the foundation for the new Singapore they wished to come about. This was a new politics. Thus, they began to see themselves no longer as nucleated individuals driven by the economic imperatives of separated lives but as a self-respecting community with honourable values and community spiritedness. To the extent that the Government failed to notice this, it was seen to have lost touch. So, there was a shift in outlook which contributed to the tide of change that was gathering momentum since the 2011 GE. The Government was hard pressed to respond. It did not know quite how.

NTUC Leadership New Role in Fostering Co-operative Enterprises in Singapore

Other organs of the state were also stirring beneath. Some sections of the National Trades Union Congress (NTUC) were restive. Those in NTUC who implemented the nuts and bolts of its successful enterprises — the taxi business, the supermarket and insurance businesses wanted to pioneer new areas of enterprise. The NTUC's huge capital resources fuelled the new ambitions. The grassroots sections of NTUC began to hear about the very successful co-operative movements in other countries, notably in Mondragon in the Basque Country of Northern Spain. The NTUC decided to send a study team to see for themselves what was happening there.

Learning from the Mondragon Experiment

The NTUC delegates were greatly surprised and inspired when they saw the Mondragon Experiment. Mondragon is a fiercely independent culture; it celebrates the ethic of self-reliance. From very poor circumstances after World War II, its founders built up a series of very successful co-operatives.

Started in 1956 from humble beginnings, Mondragon is today the largest and most successful co-operative enterprise in Europe. It has a 100,000-strong workforce in 27 worker-owned and operated co-operative enterprises. The worker-owners hire and fire their managers evaluating them at annual General Assemblies. They have their own bank, supermarket network which has expanded into Spain and Europe, their own university, research labs and schools for their children. They have their own pension scheme and share profits according to a point system which they decide for themselves. They provide jobs for life for their members. Changes in economic prospects do not result in layoffs but in redeployment to other co-operatives and/or assignment to skills re-education courses that lead to subsequent reassignment. Relocation costs are borne by the central co-operative. Too good to be true, economists who came to evaluate and measure their output efficiency are astounded that theirs is much higher than that of comparable propriety enterprises elsewhere. Productivity is higher per worker because they work happy. Asked if they were communists, their reply is that they are not ideological but are just being practical. They have shown that they can function in the capitalist environment of Spain and the European Union. An American team from the United Steelworkers union studied the Mondragon Model and tried to adapt it to the United States of America with some success.

Revamped Educational Institutions

It has long been acknowledged that creative intelligence, diligence and resolute application are the keys to Singapore's success, hence the emphasis on education from the beginning. These took the forms of compulsory schooling, a multi-track path through ITEs, polytechnics and finally to the universities in a vast integrated network that served Singapore well in its time. As new challenges emerged in the wake of the global slowdown, a twist in the system became necessary.

Manpower planning and education was always integrated. When the manpower planners re-did their labour force projections, they began to take into account a 600,000 potential Singaporean workforce which was hitherto left out of their calculations. They found that if there was a change in the education system by introducing the German work/study system into schools and even in higher education, this would liberate many 16 to 24-year olds into the workforce productively. Moreover, if spatially, schools and training institutions were reconceived and disaggregated and located into the new HDB Smart Webs, there would be multiple advantages in efficiency and knowledge acquisition. Finally, if the National Service military stint was shortened to one and a half years with the balance of one year devoted to working for points which count towards Co-curricular Activity (CCA) credits required in higher education and in the enrichment of job *curricula vitae*, there would be a significant boost to the needed workforce with the added advantage of students having work experience and a mature sense of realism as well.

Character Education

In line with these moves, school education also got a boost in its drive towards including character development in its curriculum. Hitherto character education was hard to fit into the largely book-based learning system and refocusing this meant character development became the core curriculum. Education thus became holistic through the introduction of the new 5Cs — Courage, Curiosity, Creativity, Compassion and Collaborative ability and these values replaced the old materialistic and selfish 5Cs which were previously touted as Cash, Condo, Credit Card, Country Club and Car. A much deeper level of personal and community motivation came about.

The boost to education was through recruiting suitable teachers from all over the world in addition to talented and passionate locals into our schools and universities, the polytechnics and the ITE as well. At last, this was the new foundation put in place after years of tweaking the education system.

Changes in the Civil Service

A major transformation that led to the "new" civil service and "new" government came into existence after the 2016 GE. In line with the revamping of the physical space of Singapore through the "Southern Intensification" plan and the insertion of Smart Webs into all HDB estates, the changes in the educational institutions as well as the People's Association and community centres also underwent radical review. Community centres ceased to be a point location but became a "network Community Centre System". Schools and the ITE also became "distributed learning webs" integrated into the HDB Smart Webs.

Unlike the "hub and spoke" concept within the old mechanical model, schools were no longer seen as a centralised cluster of facilities but as a web of classrooms, laboratories, halls, lecture theatres and libraries meshed into the communities they serve. Inserted into the larger intelligent HDB webs, they contributed to it and benefitted from it as well. There was much synergy and economy achieved through co-location. For example, school canteens could either be open to the public or food could be obtained from nearby food centres for mutual benefit. These were some of the obvious synergies obtained along with many other activities such as with sports, in the arts and the use of classrooms by the community. Empty classrooms would serve the purposes of adult education in the evenings, holidays and weekends, and so would the empty assembly halls and the like.

Ageing in Place with Dignity and Purpose

Those aged 55 to 75 years old who were previously regarded as marginal to the workforce found new life.

Through job redesign and co-locating jobs within the Smart Webs in HDB estates, retirees found satisfying jobs close to where they lived. They also received special skills training in the Smart Web, rubbing shoulders with school-going kids and being at the heart of things. Rather than languishing in the assigned old folks' corners, they found dignity and livelihood in many new occupations — tending to organic vegetable and herb farms in the public spaces, in jobs found in the decentralised health-care facilities, supervising the local traffic, running local community micro-credit banks, providing cultural and educational inputs through their accounts of time spent with school children, running the local libraries, managing the post offices, food centres and so on. The retirees want to be useful and thus respected, and they want to live near their friends and family. These could all be achieved in and near the Smart Webs.

Survivability and Creativity

Survivability and creativity are twin concepts. The talent pool in Singapore is needed to ride through the tough economic times. The timely implementation of the Smart Web in the HDB estates combined with the work or study, character-development-centred education system at all levels of learning has put Singapore in good stead for the uncertain future that it has to face. 2022 was no different from 2012 in that sense. The uncertainties and the vulnerability of Singapore are a constant. Survivability of Singapore is premised on its total intelligence. This is what was achieved in the 10 years from 2012 to 2022.

All these changes were added into the Smart Webs in the HDB estates. ITE Version 2, Polytechnics Version 2, Schools Version 2, Community Centres Version 2 were all spread along the Smart Webs and together with commercial and other facilities created the pedagogical environment.

Together with the Southern Intensification Plan, pressure on the rest of the island abated. The population stabilised at 6.5 million and the transformation of the HDB estates with the insertion of

Smart Webs raised the entire level of intelligence of the population. They were also happier. The total fertility rate began to rise even as the size of the ageing population climbed. Singapore, having survived the Global Financial Crisis also became the new creative centre of Asia...

Chapter 7

A Narrative for Winning*

Viswa Sadasivan

* This article was originally published in Commentary, Volume 23 titled "Singapore Challenged: The Uneasy and Unchartered Road Ahead" Viswa Sadasivan is the Chief Executive Officer of Strategic Moves, a corporate strategy, strategic and crisis communication consultancy, and training firm. He was a Nominated Member of Parliament (NMP) from 2010 to 2012.

Of the lessons in political commentary that the late S Chandramohan taught me, one stands out. He was then the Director of the Current Affairs Programmes Division of the Singapore Broadcasting Corporation. In the draft of my script for a special edition of the then popular weekly current affairs programme, *Feedback*, I described the former Prime Minister (PM) Mr Lee Kuan Yew as a "politician". Chandra told me that I was wrong; the term "politician" is pejorative and refers to those who use political power to further interests that are less than noble. He said that Singapore has political leaders who have the "intellectual sophistication and emotional integrity" to deliver on promises. Chandra emphasised that even though some of their policies and actions could appear undemocratic and even draconian, closer examination would show that they were based on a "logic of accountability".

This logic, in turn, is based on a "social contract" between the Government and the people — an understanding that in return for prosperity and progress, the people agree to hard work, government control and reduced freedom. The crucial point, Chandra explained, was that this agreement was predicated on a deep and mutual acceptance of a "socio-political narrative" that defines who we are, what we stand for, where we have come from, and where we would like to be.

So what was this narrative? There were two national narratives created in the 1960s. The first was the narrative for merger with Malaya:

> We are a small country with no natural resources and limited human capability — survival is possible only if we compensate for that which we lack by merging with a larger, more established country. We will benefit from a common market, having a hinterland and the security of a more established armed force. It would be a bonus if we merged with a country with which we already have cultural and kinship ties. Malaya fits the bill.

This narrative unified a series of compelling arguments that were presented to the people during the 1963 campaign leading to the People's Action Party (PAP) Government's victory in the referendum on Singapore's merger with Malaya. The narrative was used as leverage to create a collective reflex not only amongst a disparate people, but also between the people and the Government. It deepened trust in the ruling party and helped build faith in PM Lee's leadership and vision.

In fact, this faith became so entrenched in the months that followed that it withstood the ultimate test when Singapore was unceremoniously severed from the Federation of Malaysia. Virtually overnight, the merger narrative went up in smoke. Clearly, part of the reason why PM Lee was highly emotional during the televised press conference on 9 August, 1965 was the loss of face in having to backtrack on all he had said before to persuade the people that merger was the only way for Singapore to survive.

This must certainly constitute a rare occurrence in political history when a narrative that was imbibed by the people had to be dismantled and promptly replaced by another narrative promulgated by the same leader! This is usually the recipe for the ignominious demise of a political leader. It was clearly not so in the case of Mr Lee and the PAP Government.

The new post-Independence narrative worked for three reasons: the political leadership had already established a credible level of trust with the people by delivering on promises made since 1959; the leaders saw it as their duty to walk the ground day and night to persuade the people to accept the Government's agenda and belief system; and perhaps most importantly, the new narrative capitalised on the prevailing sense of having been abandoned and was, therefore, emotionally relevant and compelling.

The new narrative had to serve two purposes: it had to get the people to stand, unquestioning, behind their leaders, and it had to be a clarion call for charging ahead towards success, almost to prove a point to detractors and to ourselves.

If Mr Lee and his "lieutenants" were the captain and the crew of the ship that sailed the rough seas, carrying us in it, the new narrative was the wind behind the sail.

This narrative formed the basis of the much talked-about "social contract" that gave the Government the licence to rule with minimal resistance from the ground. Also, with the new narrative that was predicated on faith, the Government had the latitude to go with its instincts when sailing into the unchartered waters of the 1960s and 70s. Starting from scratch and forced to blaze new trails for a nation in-the-making, the political leaders often had to lead with messianic zeal! Together with a team of able public servants, they systematically and painstakingly built key institutions such as the Economic Development Board (EDB), the Monetary Authority of Singapore (MAS) and the Housing and Development Board (HDB).

What connected them was their fervent belief in the new Singapore narrative, which was essentially this:

> We have become independent and can rely only on ourselves. We have learned that dependence comes with a price. The hard truth is that countries act to protect their own interests. We are small, vulnerable and have no natural resources. Our survival depends on rapidly building 'core muscles' — our economy, security and social compact. Our small size can be our strength — like a sampan, tossed about on rough seas, nimble enough to quickly change course, unlike an ocean liner. We must embrace pragmatism. Our mantra — Hard-work and Discipline. We must be prepared to sacrifice for the future, and this includes personal freedoms and liberties. Meritocracy and equal opportunities will be our governing principles. To this end, the government will relentlessly seek new solutions and provide a good home for the people. In return, the people need to follow faithfully. This is our social contract. We cannot be limited by what we have, but must be galvanised by what we can become — a success story that will silence our detractors, and inspire future generations. There is no reason why we can't achieve this. We need to believe.

To illustrate the inimitable mood in the Singapore of the 1960s as well as the unquestioning faith that comes with being fully invested in a narrative, here is an often-recounted conversation that took place in the 1960s between American economist and Nobel Laureate, Milton Friedman and former Cabinet minister, S Dhanabalan, who was then a senior economist with the EDB:

"Friedman: What are you going to do now that you have lost the Malaysian Common Market?

Dhanabalan: We don't know what we're going to do but I want to assure you that if you came back in 10 years' time, you will see that we have succeeded.

Friedman: What kind of answer is that for an economist?

Dhanabalan: I'm sorry but the truth is, we have not the slightest clue what we will or should do. We just have the will and the determination. We will not only survive, we will prosper."

This indomitable belief with which the leaders led, was matched by the faith with which the people followed the Government. This was the basis for the "social contract" which was at the core of the narrative.

This contributed to the socio-economic progress and prosperity of the first three decades since Independence in 1965. The people's willingness to suspend civil liberties for economic progress allowed leaders to get away with what would have been deemed seriously politically incorrect in most contexts. Take these remarks made by PM Lee Kuan Yew in his 1983 National Day Rally speech:

> If you don't include your women graduates in your breeding pool and leave them on the shelf, you would end up a more stupid society...So what happens? There will be less bright people to support dumb people in the next generation. That's a problem.

There were no consequences for PM Lee or the PAP Government. They continued to ride on the power of the post-Independence narrative. However, time does not stand still. Circumstances change and people change — so must narratives.

The PAP Government's reluctance to reshape the narrative was a significant contributor to, what I see as, a gradual erosion of its stature and standing in the eyes of the people from the 1990s till May of 2011.

With affluence, better education and greater exposure, Singaporeans became less willing to accept everything that the Government did or said. Having benefited from a better quality of life, the appetite for issues of fairness, right and wrong, and justice grew steadily. Singaporeans not only started having opinions, but also developed a desire for expressing them. The Internet provided the platform for this. The gap between the people and the Government narrowed. The old "social contract" had reached its run-out-date.

However, the PAP Government failed to see the need to develop a fresh, concrete and equally potent national narrative and "sell it" with the same evangelistic fervour as it did in the 1960s. One could argue that with all the noise generated on the Internet and the heterogeneous nature of society today, it is far more difficult to pitch a narrative that will be received without some measure of ambivalence. Yes, it is more difficult, but not impossible. There are three prerequisites: acknowledging that ground sensibilities have shifted; discerning the deeper concerns from the symptoms; and having the interest and will to change the governing approach.

"Tweaking" the system or making incremental changes do not work when people have been waiting a long time for the Government to not just listen, but demonstrate that it is listening. What is needed is a bold and distinctly different new narrative that is unequivocal in substance and articulated persuasively in one voice by the leaders — one that not only strikes a chord with the people but is also something the Government is capable of and committed to delivering.

Failing to acknowledge the growing discord between the Government and the people's sensibilities invariably has consequences. Take Mr Lee Kuan Yew's off-side remark during the hustings of the 2011 General Election on the consequences if the Aljunied Group Representation Constituency (GRC) were to go to the Opposition:

> ...If Aljunied decides to go that way, well Aljunied has five years to live and repent....

This remark in the language of the old narrative, spoken with misplaced confidence that the people continued to have unquestioning faith in their political leaders was, many believe, the single most significant factor that led to the PAP losing Aljunied GRC in 2011. The electoral result and the reaction of the populace to the remark amounted to a summary rejection of the post-Independence narrative. Never before had the signal been clearer.

Since May 2011, we have seen a discernible shift in the way the Government operates. It clearly appears to be listening and responding more. The Government is more prepared than ever before to re-examine issues that were considered taboo or at least indulgent in the old narrative: direct assistance for the needy, HDB flats for singles, and more help for special needs schools. There has also been a dramatic, almost uncanny, improvement in the Government's ability to address and solve problems, especially with housing and transportation. These have helped the Government regain faith. We have also seen a multifold increase in public and stakeholder engagements, further demonstrating the Government's willingness to listen to the people. In addition, the PM, virtually all Cabinet ministers and PAP MPs have a presence on Facebook. In short, there has been a profusion of "conversations" since the 2011 General Election.

However, we have yet to "see" a distinct new narrative emerge. Perhaps PM Lee Hsien Loong's 2013 National Day Rally speech came closest to articulating it. As long as we do not hear a compelling new narrative, the Government will continue to be identified with the post-Independence narrative. This is likely to alienate today's populace, especially the young.

The Government's reluctance to move away decisively from the old narrative of three decades is understandable, especially since it has produced tangible results. The new narrative does not need to be a total rejection of the old one. For example, meritocracy, equal opportunities, efficiency, and even having a strong, decisive government, are all qualities that most Singaporeans still value. What is important is that the core of the new narrative must resonate strongly with the defining considerations of the people today — our identity, a sense of fairness and justice, balancing progress and prosperity with equitable opportunities and aspirations, and a more partnership-based principle of governance.

In short, a good narrative is one that addresses three factors: it must be in sync with the logic of the audience and stakeholders;

there must be a clear sense of empathy for the people's core concerns; and it must be congruous with the ethical considerations of the day.

The sooner a coherent and bold new narrative is designed in a way that resonates with ground sensibilities, the better chance of gaining a buy-in from the people. This is the best way to move out of the current level of flux and find a new operating equilibrium. Like societies, organisations which have taken pains to develop a powerful narrative that goes beyond stating what they do well, to defining what they stand for, have found success. After all, mind-share is the basis for sustainable market share. Similarly, in an increasingly competitive marketplace, product or price differentiation has limited scope — people increasingly want to be associated with products, concepts and ideals that make them feel good.

This is what differentiates the men from the boys, so to speak — a certain maturity and sophistication in defining what your organisation stands for. The Body Shop stands firmly against animal testing, Apple for innovation boldness, and AirAsia pushes a revolution in the region where "now everyone can fly". These are not iconic organisations merely flashing clever slogans. The sentiments conveyed by these catchphrases are at the core of the narrative of the organisation — something that unifies the sensibilities of the internal and external stakeholders. This, in turn, engenders loyalty, which is an increasingly elusive concept today.

The National University of Singapore (NUS) has systematically moved up the global rankings over the past decade. In its earlier years, it focused on being a good teaching university. In the past seven years, the differentiator has shifted to research. In a few years, NUS may very well get into the top 20 list. Teaching, research and facilities will be mere hygiene factors then. Universities in this "club" talk more about what they stand for, such as the fascinating ways their faculty, alumni and students contribute to making this a better, more exciting world. Why the university has decided on its course and its causes and how committed it is to them, form the core of the narrative which is imbued in every member of the university family. This creates pride of association.

Mission and vision statements are static descriptions of what you do and aspire to achieve. In most cases, these fail to capture the imagination of stakeholders because they do not usually present the context — they do not tell us where you started, why you decided on this course, what trials you faced in your journey, what kept you going, what your final destination is, and why this is important for you and your people.

If we examine greatness — The Roman Empire, The Taj Mahal, Nelson Mandela, The Ford Corporation, The Beatles, Mahatma Gandhi, The French Revolution and Singapore — the common factor would be the strength of the narrative. People have always rallied behind ideas and ideals, more than products and services. Today, with so much devastation and disillusionment, with all the noise and single-minded aimlessness, the search for what is meaningful that gives hope and is authentic has intensified.

More than ever, the narrative is key — those who have the instinct for it are the true winners.

Chapter 8

The New Singapore Dream*

Kishore Mahbubani

*This article was originally published in Commentary, Volume 23 titled "The Uneasy and Unchartered Road Ahead" © 2014 The National University of Singapore Society. Professor Kishore Mahbubani is Distinguished Fellow at the Asia Research Institute of the National University of Singapore, and former Dean of the Lee Kuan Yew School of Public Policy, at the same university.

It is always best to begin an article with a strong statement to grab the reader's attention. So here is my strong statement: when Singapore celebrates its 50th anniversary on 9 August 2015, it can confidently claim that no other newly independent nation has developed as rapidly and as comprehensively as Singapore has in its first 50 years. Several people have challenged this claim of mine. However, when asked to name any other newly independent nation that has done better than Singapore, they could not. In short, for the first 50 years of its development, Singapore can lay claim to having been number one in the world.

Allow me to make my second strong statement: if Singapore continues on autopilot and repeats the same goals and policies as it had in its first 50 years, it will be heading towards disaster. Bluntly put, the goals and policies that have worked in the first 50 years will not work for the subsequent 50 years. And why not? The simple answer is that the world has changed. Singapore too, must change. In the first 50 years, Singapore had the first-mover advantage. We were ahead of the rest of the world and our region in adopting policies which propelled us forward. Today, the rest of the world and our region have begun copying our best practices. If we play the same game, we will be left behind. Therefore, we have to start playing new games.

To begin playing new games, we may need to have a new set of aspirations. Clearly, the early generations of Singaporeans (including mine) wanted to get out of poverty and enjoy the fruits of prosperity. This was the reason for going for the five Cs: cars, condominiums, cash, credit cards and country club memberships. However, if all 5 million residents of Singapore keep pushing for the five Cs, we may well have an island that is uninhabitable.

Let me state at the outset that there is no restriction on the amount of cash or credit cards which Singaporeans can acquire. Here, there are no finite limits. However, given the fact that we are one of the smallest countries in the world, and, after Monaco, the most densely populated member state of the United Nations (UN), it is impossible for Singapore to satisfy the demands of each and every citizen and resident in the areas of cars, condominiums and country clubs. Singapore does not and cannot have the physical space to provide these goods to everyone.

To date, Singapore has designed very good public policies which have raised the prices of finite goods such as cars to ensure that they remain out of the reach of most Singaporeans. However, while demand has been squeezed by higher prices, there has been no discernible effort to address the underlying factors propelling demand. Even today, no middle-class Singaporean believes that he has "arrived" until he owns a car, even though a car in Singapore is outrageously expensive by global standards. In short, a car remains an essential part of the Singaporean Dream. Yet, if every Singaporean achieves his or her dream, we will have a national nightmare on-hand.

To prevent this national nightmare, we have created harsher policies to reduce the demand for cars. Paradoxically, the higher prices of cars have made them even more desirable as status symbols. This is the reason for luxury brands trumping cheap brands in Singapore. If the desirability of cars continue to rise, our efforts to curtail car ownership will be as successful as a dog chasing its tail. Moreover, if we keep alive the Singaporean Dream of owning a car and restrict access to that dream, we will inevitably create a disgruntled and frustrated middle class. Indeed, this may be one reason for the rising levels of unhappiness in Singapore. Many Singaporeans feel that their incomes are rising, yet they feel that the Singaporean Dream of cars, condominiums and country clubs is receding rather than getting closer. The stark contrast between Singapore and the developed world makes this clearer. In 2010, there were 477 cars for every 1,000 individuals in the European Union (EU), the highest ratio in the world. In contrast in Singapore, there are 117 cars for every 1,000 individuals.

So what then is the solution? The solution is obvious: change the Singaporean Dream! Yes, almost every Singaporean reading this article will laugh at this suggestion. How can well-off Singaporeans deprive themselves of owning cars? It provides the most reliable form of transportation as well as a powerful status symbol. The minute one owns a car, especially a Mercedes, BMW or Lexus, friends will know that you have "arrived".

I have lived 10 years of my life on another "even more crowded" tiny island where it is not rational to drive or own a car. In fact, it is considered downright foolish to buy and own a car if one lives in Manhattan. All this hit home one evening in Manhattan when I saw the former chairman of Citibank, Walter Wriston and his wife, Kathryn, standing on First Avenue with their arms raised and attempting to hail a cab. Clearly, Walter Wriston was a very wealthy man. He could have easily bought a car (cars are cheap in Manhattan) and parked it anywhere he liked (even though parking charges in Manhattan are among the highest in the world). Yet, it just did not make sense. The ecosystem of public transport in Manhattan developed into a combination of subway trains, public buses and readily-accessible taxis. This meant that, in a crunch, you could get anywhere within Manhattan easily by taking public transport. Meanwhile, the hassle of driving and high costs of parking in downtown Manhattan meant that owning and using a car made even less sense. Significantly, Mayor Michael Bloomberg, one of the richest Americans, used to take a subway train to work in Manhattan. Former Bogota Mayor Enrique Peñalosa put it succinctly, "A developed country is not a place where the poor have cars; it's where the rich use public transportation."

Therefore, the new Singaporean solution is to dream a happier dream. We have to give up this "insane" dream of wanting to rely on a car and replace it with an ecosystem of a public transport which would make it irrational to own a car. Such an ecosystem will include a reliable and resilient Mass Rapid Transit (MRT) system and a frequent bus service, taxis available especially when it thunders and showers and pools of electric cars ready for rental. This failure to provide such a public transport ecosystem is probably one of Singapore's biggest in its first 50 years of development. We have succeeded in creating the world's best port, the world's best airport and the world's best airline, just to name a few. Hence, we understand the game of logistics and transportation well. Since Singapore is one of the world's most densely-populated countries, we should have been able to apply the same degree of knowledge, skills and expertise so that our public transport system would have developed as Singapore developed.

We could have done it right and did come close to doing so. When I served as Singapore's Ambassador to the UN from 1984 to 1989, my American counterpart was the legendary Ambassador Vernon A. Walters. During his globe spanning travels, his hobby was to investigate the MRT system of every city he visited. He proudly told me that he could confidently declare that the Singapore MRT system was the best in the world. I asked him why and his reply was that it was the only MRT system in the world that had been built ahead of schedule, below cost and operated smoothly.

So the million-dollar question is: What went wrong? Did we choose the wrong people or the wrong policies to build our public transport system? There is no doubt that we can have a vigorous debate in response to this question and we could have many different answers. However, there is no simple and correct answer. Each answer in turn reflects an opinion based on a set of values. So, I would not be surprised if my simple answer is taken as controversial as well.

I personally believe that the fundamental mistake which Singapore made in the area of public transport was to allow ideological considerations to trump pragmatic considerations. We made three critical ideological errors. Firstly, we assumed that companies motivated by profits were more efficient at delivering public goods than government bodies. Hence, we privatised the public transport system. We trusted the profit motive more than government efficiency in delivering public goods such as public transport.

The second error was to compound the first by insisting that each limb of the public transport system had to be profitable. The MRT and bus companies had to ultimately make money. Indeed, for a while, each new MRT line had to be viable, alongside the taxi companies. Yet, we also pay taxes for a good public transport system and we collect a huge sum annually from vehicle-related car taxes, fees and charges. Why not use some of it to deliver better public services starting with better public transport?

The third ideological error was to assume that Singaporeans would never give up their tradition of "car worship". As cars became more costly, we too, paradoxically turned the car into an even bigger status symbol. In spending more money on roads, tunnels and flyovers to ensure freer flow of traffic, we actually created a transport ecosystem which rewarded driving versus using public transport. Indeed, several urban planners have made the case that traffic will expand and fill any available road space. This is why way back in 1957, the respected American urbanist Lewis Mumford advocated construction on the Interstate Highway System be suspended for two years entirely.

The real solution to Singapore's public transport woes is to challenge some of these basic, underlying assumptions. Let us examine them in reverse order. Firstly, we can change the culture of "car worship". Ironically, Singapore has been very good at various forms of social engineering. At the point of Singapore's independence, there was a culture of corruption. There was also a culture of heavy smoking. It would be fair to say that Singapore has reduced both corruption and heavy smoking. In the 1970s, 26 percent of Singaporeans were smokers. From then, it declined to 22 percent in 1983, 18.3 percent in 1992 and 14.3 percent in 2010. The point we have learned from behavioural economics is that it is possible to change human behaviour by shaping social norms in desired directions. Having succeeded in other areas, could we not make a conscious decision to change the culture and cult of "car worship" in Singapore?

However, to succeed in persuading Singaporeans to reduce their dependence on cars, we must in turn deliver a public transport system that is among the best in the world. Today, with the availability of big data, we can find out where people want to go at different points in time. Instead of mechanically creating bus routes which only ply certain set routes at certain fixed times of the day, we can anticipate demand and deliver public transport that responds acutely to micro-level demand data. Of course, this means that not every "limb" of the public transport system will be profitable. Instead of looking at the "profitability" of each "limb", we should conduct an overall examination of our public transport system and ask ourselves a simple question: Is the system as a whole delivering the public good it is designed to? And can we use a combination of fee collection and car taxes to pay for the public transport system? If we are able to, then we will have gotten rid of one of the main local sources of public dissatisfaction locally.

Finally, we have to get rid of a final set of ideological blinkers to solve our public transport problem. This means that we have to stop "worshipping" the private sector and to stop believing that the private sector can do a better job than the public sector in delivering public goods. In this area, we need to develop a higher degree of intellectual honesty. We should be honest and admit that like the rest of the world we were misled by the Reagan-Thatcher ideological revolution and we believed that the private sector is inherently better than the public sector in delivering all kinds of goods, including public goods. One of the great strengths of the "Singaporean approach" to problem-solving was that we claimed to be rational and pragmatic. Yet, as a result of becoming prisoners of the Reagan-Thatcher ideology, we made deeply flawed decisions that inevitably damaged our delivery of public services.

Let me offer a striking example that has been mentioned by several retired permanent secretaries. They have said that it was a mistake to privatise the Public Works Department (PWD). This Department contained a lot of valuable knowledge, skills and experience which could have helped Singapore with a lot of its engineering and development challenges. Sadly, when PWD was sold off first to Temasek Holdings and then to an Australian company Downer Edi, and subsequently to China Architecture Design and Research Group, Singapore lost all the skills and experience we had built up over the years.

To the best of my knowledge, we have never publicly admitted that we made a mistake in selling off the PWD. The time has come to do so now. The goal of such an admission is not to assign blame to any public officers: it would be pointless to do so. Instead, such an admission could liberate our minds from the ideological assumptions of the Reagan-Thatcher revolution and open our minds to the possibility that sometimes the public sector is best at providing public goods.

Once we accept that premise, we would have laid the critical intellectual foundation on which an excellent ecosystem of public transport can be built. We can begin to collect big data on the potential demand for all the "limbs" and "arteries" of such an ecosystem. We can then systematically build a total system that at least tries to meet every aspect of this demand. Clearly, some of the "limbs" will be economically profitable. Other "limbs" will be less profitable or even unprofitable. It may however still be necessary to have these unprofitable "limbs". And, the reason? Because we are providing a public service, not a private good.

To understand this critical notion of a public service, think of our postal service. We buy 26-cent stamps to post a letter to any where within Singapore. It is profitable for the post office to deliver mail to Housing and Development Board (HDB) estates because the mailboxes are situated close together making delivery easy. It is unprofitable or less profitable to deliver letters to Good Class Bungalow (GCB) areas because the mailboxes are far apart. It costs the post office much more to deliver mail to private housing areas than to HDB estates. However, it delivers equally everywhere. Why is this so? Because mail service is a public service.

Similarly, like the postal service, public transport should be perceived as a public service. We should endeavour to provide it to all the citizens and residents of the island, even if some parts of the system may experience less cost recovery than others. Here, we should take full advantage of the fact that we are one of the smallest countries in the world with no vast distances to cover. Indeed, if any leading experts on public transport in the world were looking for an ideal public policy laboratory to try out best practices and new ideas with public transport, they could find no better site than Singapore. Here all the critical factors are in place to build the world's best ecosystem of public transport.

Thus, when we do so, the rational and pragmatic Singaporeans will progressively give up their dream of owning cars. It was perfectly reasonable for my generation of Singaporeans to aspire for the materialistic five Cs. Many of us grew up in poverty and believed that happiness only came with more and more material acquisitions.

Now we know better. As most Singaporeans have satisfied their basic material needs, and more, there is less and less of a need to accumulate material goods. Indeed, according to Maslow's hierarchy of needs, we will get more satisfaction and happiness as we pay more attention to the higher order needs of love or belonging, esteem and self-actualisation.

We are truly blessed that, for the most part, the basic physical and intellectual infrastructure is in place in Singapore to enable most Singaporeans to lead a good life. Indeed, we should all continue working hard but what are we working for? We can work towards a future when the former five Cs become less and less important. We can begin by dropping the dream of the idea that having cars will produce happiness.

Chapter 9

Singapore in Transition: Staying Together for the Next 50 — Reviving the National Language*

Yang Razali Kassim

*This article was originally published in Commentary, Volume 24 titled "Singapore @ 50: Reflections and Observations" © 2015 The National University of Singapore Society. The late Yang Razali Kassim was a Senior Fellow at S. Rajaratnam School of International Studies, Nanyang Technological University, Singapore. He was Chairman of the Association of Muslim Professionals and a career journalist.

Pondering the Way Forward

On the 60th anniversary of the National University of Singapore Society (NUSS) on 3 October 2014, Prime Minister (PM) Lee Hsien Loong spoke of Singapore in transition. For the next phase in its evolution as a nation-state, he said that three basic principles would be needed: first, looking out to stay plugged in to the world while looking in on domestic challenges; second, being good hearted while remaining hard headed; and third, understanding our past as we embrace the future.

"We are now at an inflexion point, changing gears, changing pace. We need not only to navigate the eddies and currents from moment to moment, but to keep in mind basic principles which will help us maintain our momentum, our direction, our purpose," said PM Lee as he sketched broad strokes of what would be needed for the next journey. Essentially, these would be the guiding fundamentals, the details of which presumably would be for Singaporeans to identify, debate and forge a new consensus on, as we stand on the cusp of marking the 50th anniversary of Singapore's independence in 2015. In other words, for the next phase of Singapore's maturing as a nation-state, we must bear in mind certain basic fundamentals. This, to me, is key to our way forward.

However, what should the basic principles be? And what of the past must we not discard as we march into the future? Now that we are at these critical crossroads, what PM Lee called "an inflexion point", we have to decide on the kind of Singapore we want over the next 50 years. How different, or similar, will the new Singapore be from the Singapore that we have known for the past five decades? How much familiarity from the past do we want to retain to avoid a sense of rupture with our own history?

In my view, for the next 50 years, this sense of continuity amid change helps Singapore stabilise its journey forward. Indeed, as I see it, this anchor rests on three legs, all intertwined and mutually reinforcing. All three played their respective roles in the last 50 years to forge a common consciousness out of the disparate ethnic communities. Will the three legs — national identity, multiracialism and the national language — remain central to the future nation- state? Will they remain pillars of the future, and if not, why not?

National Identity in Transition?

It is significant that, at this inflexion point, PM Lee sees Singapore as a nation in transition. However, what does this mean? Does it suggest that everything about Singapore is in transition? Does it also mean that Singapore's national identity — of being Singaporean — is in a stage of transition? If so, what would the end state or future state be? At the same time, a state of transition implies some flux or some uncertainty. If so, perhaps the time has come for Singaporeans to discuss and renew the national consensus on our national identity. It is in this regard that PM Lee's notion of the basic principles and the intertwining of the past and the future become crucial as we ponder our way forward.

Since Independence, our national identity has revolved around the interaction of the main ethnic communities of the Chinese, Malays, Indians and Eurasians, as well as others. Singapore's first Prime Minister, Lee Kuan Yew, understood instantly the crucial need to forge a common identity out of the disparate communities. Although Singapore was predominantly Chinese, its Malay origin is a historical and geopolitical fact that could not be ignored. Lee was acutely aware of the history and geopolitics of the emerging nation-state. Hence, its road to national identity which inevitably took into account the forging of a fine balance among the major races, had two distinct phases.

The first phase was defined by the drive to merge with Malaya to form Malaysia in 1963. Synchronising Singapore's identity politics with Malaysia therefore made political sense — but the Malaysia arrangement was short-lived. With the nation's independence in 1965, Lee's Singapore had to forge a brand new national identity — a "Singaporean" Singapore. In this second phase, the new identity adapted to the post-Independence political reality without completely detaching from the past. A core aspect of this new national identity was multiracialism and was reflected in the parity of the four official cultures and their languages — English, Malay, Chinese and Tamil. However, with English as the working language, making Malay the national language was a strategic step. More than a mother tongue of Singapore's largest minority group, Malay would be the unifying language of the emergent independent Singapore — The national anthem, commands and insignias of the uniformed services, national awards are all in Malay. These symbolisms aside, much else was in English, the language of administration.

As Lee put it to a panel of journalists on 11 August 1965, two days after Independence, "The pledge given by the People's Action Party (PAP) is not for the purposes of getting votes. We will earnestly carry it out. I make this promise: this is not a Chinese country. Singapore is not a Chinese country, nor a Malay country nor an Indian country..." On 19 December 1966, speaking at the opening of a school, Lee added, "But to each also must be given the maximum of common denominators without which you and I will never be able to understand each other...And so it is we have designated that Malay should be our national language."

Enshrined in the Constitution, the national language provided the potential glue that goes to the soul of who we are as Singaporeans. We are, as Lee said, not a Chinese state despite the majority being ethnic Chinese, nor a Malay state despite Singapore's historically Malay origin, nor an Indian state — We are a Singaporean nation-state. Binding us together in a fine balance gave Singaporeans a sense of mutual accommodation and convergence, engendering a sense of stability and commonality as the people developed the economy and transformed Singapore from Third World to First.

In the first 50 years of nationhood, the different ethnic groups adjusted fairly well to each other, even if it was not without problems. For the minorities, this was a good start. I remember my friends were from various races: Chinese, Malays, Indians, and Eurasians. In school, playing and studying together, we conversed in English, and occasionally for some, switched to simple, conversational Malay — there was a sense of bonding. When I went to National Service in the 1970s, we had Singaporeans from various races training together and marching to Malay commands, and had such language-defined arrangements as Hokkien platoons, English platoons and even Malay platoons. The cumulative impact was to imbibe a certain sense of solidarity among the trainees. The environment was the same when I went to university and when I started work in the 1980s, although by then, English was decidedly the common tongue. "*Apa macam!*", the simple colloquial Malay greeting of "How are you!", from a non-Malay colleague captured the bilingual mood. The ability of friends and colleagues to converse in English and simple Malay sustained the feeling of togetherness. At work, my Chinese-educated friends spoke with me in English and we enjoyed our friendly banter in it.

While Malay was the national language, the wide facility in English was the most important bridge across our ethnic and cultural divides. Everyone spoke English — the Chinese, Malays, and Indians. The Chinese, Malay and Tamil schools eventually closed down under the weight of market forces. English was also the social leveller as Singaporeans of every ethnic group spoke the language to get jobs and to communicate with each other albeit in their respective ethnic twangs. Overtime, *Singlish* developed and surged to the forefront while Malay as the national language receded further into symbolism — there was a gradual but certain shift in the socio-linguistic landscape.

The Shifting Ground

From the 1990s, I began to sense the shifting ground. Shopkeepers were either not able or not as easily inclined to break into conversational Malay. Taxi drivers asked for my destination in *Singlish* or English, and not conversational Malay anymore, unlike 10 years ago. I found myself speaking to shopkeepers and taxi drivers less and less in Malay, unlike in the past decade or two. Younger Singaporeans could be heard chatting away in Mandarin and not in English. In public places, such as on mass rapid transit (MRT) trains and in malls, the chatter was as much in Mandarin as it was in English or *Singlish.*

While this was an understandable consequence of the changed education system, I was beginning to ask myself whether a gulf was emerging as a result of the generational shift. I was beginning to worry whether the different ethnic groups were drifting apart. Yet, at the same time, I noticed that the national uniformed services, the military, police and civil defence, were still using the trappings of the national language, especially Malay for their formation commands and drills, as vividly displayed during National Day parades. Regimental sergeant majors were still called respectfully, "*Encik*" (Malay for "Sir"). Significantly, the PM still upholds the language policy of using Malay, Mandarin and English, in that order, at his National Day Rally (NDR) speeches and the PAP's main party conferences while PAP Members of Parliament (MPs) also speak Malay in parliamentary sessions.

As the NDRs are state-of-the-nation addresses widely telecast to every Singaporean home, this was clearly a deliberate policy by the national leadership to underscore the continuing importance of the three languages with Malay as the national language. Strangely, however, the announcers on television consistently referred to the PM delivering his "speech in Malay", not "speech in the national language" as it should rightly be. I was wondering whether this was a manifestation of an oversight, ignorance, or more tellingly, of the widespread social amnesia of the fact that Malay is the national language.

National Identity and Changing Demographics

While those who were quietly concerned about the perfunctory role of the national language were naturally Malays, I realised over time that this feeling was neither mine nor the community's alone. A number of my non-Malay Singaporean friends also noticed that with equal concern, and they were not just from my generation but also younger ones. For example, I discovered that a friend from a local Chinese language newspaper was taking up Malay classes. Ironically, we were then travelling together to a conference held in Beijing when she told me this. When I asked "why?", she replied "why not? — after all Malay is our national language", she said. This was a huge revelation for me — I had assumed, very wrongly, that a Singaporean from a Chinese-speaking environment would never feel any attachment to the national language. I wondered how many more Singaporeans were like her. If she was a reflection of a silent undercurrent of concern with regard to the state of the national language, then the future of social integration among Singapore's various communities in the next phase would be hopeful.

In more recent years, this concern was accentuated by the trend in immigration. As more and more foreigners took root in Singapore and became citizens as result of the Government's open-door policy, I wondered how they would integrate and imbibe core Singaporean values and identity. I also wondered whether they would be able to understand the genesis and evolution of the Singaporean ethos, including multiracialism, and the reason why the Singapore's founding fathers chose Malay as the national language. It was for this very reason that I wrote an article reflecting my concerns for the future of Singapore's national integration in this journal two years ago entitled *Imagining Singapore 2030: Language, Demographics and the Region.* My related concern was whether the changing demographics in Singapore, brought about by the growing immigration, would divide Singaporeans which heightened the need to bind ourselves even more cohesively in ways that include use of national language.

Two years later, one of Singapore's foremost public intellectuals, Kishore Mahbubani, wrote a thought-provoking commentary in his *Big Ideas* column in The Straits Times. On 14 June 2014, in his essay titled *Big Idea No 5: Speak the National Language*, he called for a campaign to revive the national language by encouraging Singaporeans to speak *Bahasa Melayu* (the Malay Language). His comment was unprecedented in its openness, frankness and clarity. I cannot recall any public figure, either Malay and non-Malay, who has so cogently and boldly made such an exhortation. He said, "Please notice I did not say 'study' the national language. Nor did I say 'read' or 'write' the national language. I only said 'speak' because we should set a very low bar and get most Singaporeans connected with their national language."

He listed five reasons, "in ascending order of importance why Singaporeans should learn to speak *Bahasa Melayu*": The first is to be a normal country because Singapore was to him an "abnormal country" as most Singaporeans did not speak their national language. Second, Singaporeans would be able to sing their national anthem with greater feeling and passion if they knew a few words of *Bahasa Melayu.* Third is the pragmatic reason of being surrounded by Malay-speaking neighbours such as Malaysia, Indonesia and Brunei. The ability to speak the same language would open up various opportunities, including economic ones. Besides, by 2030, according to one projection he cited, Indonesia may become the seventh-largest economy in the world, overtaking Britain and Germany. The fourth reason is a geopolitical one — "Most small nations survive over the longer term by developing geopolitical understanding of the neighbourhood." The final reason, "and perhaps the most important reason for speaking *Bahasa Melayu*", he said, "is that a common understanding of our national language will be one more invisible thread that will make our nation a more cohesive one".

Public Reactions

It is instructive to note how Kishore's call was received by Singaporeans who have essentially grown up not being familiar with the national language, apart from singing the national anthem. At the same time, the rise of China and consequently, the growing importance of Mandarin has confirmed the wisdom of the Government's policy of promoting the learning of Mandarin among Chinese Singaporeans. Against this backdrop, it is not surprising if sections of Singaporean society questioned the logic of Kishore's call, such as Cheang Peng Wah who, in an online response, argued instead for the learning of Chinese as a "pragmatic step" in view of China's growing influence. Yet, it could be argued that it is for this same reason that it becomes crucial to remind Singaporeans of who we are as Singaporeans first and foremost. It is also precisely due to the potential uncertainties of the next 50 years that there is a need for a centripetal pull towards the centre, a pull which the national language is best poised to achieve.

Significantly, there appears also to be resonance among non-Malay Singaporeans who supported Kishore's urging for the use of Malay as the national language. For instance, on 24 Nov 2014, *The Straits Times* ran a letter by Jong Ching Yee calling on Singaporeans to pick up Malay as a third conversational language for social interaction in Singapore's multiracial society and as a link with the region. Echoing Jong's call, Paul Sim Ruiqi, writing on the same forum page, called for learning of the national language as a bridge to a deeper understanding of local history and culture. Taking this call further, late last year, another reader, Lee Yong Se, called on the Government to promote the revival of the national language and to ride on the momentum of Singapore's 50th anniversary celebrations to do this: "As we celebrate SG50 next year, my wish is that more non-Malay Singaporeans, especially new citizens, would be well-versed in the national language."

This growing realisation of the unifying role of the national language was noted by the Government. Speaking at the launch of the Malay Language Month for 2014, Deputy PM Tharman Shanmugaratnam said, "Malay is our national language and the Malay culture is a part of our common heritage and identity." The chairman of the organising committee who is also a senior minister of state, Masagos Zulkifli, said that he noted the growing interest of late among non-Malay Singaporeans in learning Malay and that this was a positive development as Malay could function as a "facilitator of friendly ties" in Singapore's multiracial society.

Role of the Government and the Malay Community

So what can be done? To begin with, there is a need for a study on the thinking of Singaporeans, after 50 years of Independence, on how the national language can be better positioned in the next phase of Singapore's evolution as a nation-state. In this context, there are three key determining factors: national society, the Government and the Malay community.

There will come a time when Singaporeans will feel the void, or to paraphase Kishore's statement, the "abnormality" of Singapore where there is a national language but the people do not speak it. To many, this situation has arisen due to the lack of active government policy to promote the national language, quite apart from retaining it in symbolic form at the parade square, at NDRs or PAP conferences. Views from the ground have indeed emerged on the way forward. One Straits Times reader, Roland Seow, responding to Kishore's call, proposed to "bring back *Bahasa Melayu* as a subject in school" while another Singaporean, Alan Kiong, appealed to "please make this a national policy". Bringing back the national language is clearly a major exercise in uplifting the national spirit. As Wong Wee Nam wrote in Sgpolitics.net in 2011, "There must be a conscious attempt to promote the national language. People must be reminded that there is a national language." An annual national language month could be held where free classes could be organised for those who wish to learn the language, he said. Wong's idea was echoed three years later by Wan Hussin Zoohri, a former PAP MP and teacher, when he proposed a Malay Language Week for non-Malay Singaporeans. During this period, he said the Malay Language Council of Singapore could tap non-Malay students learning Malay as a third language to display their proficiency to the public. "Such initiatives are not only appropriate and timely, but could also provide the impetus for government support."

The Malay community must also play its part. The national language must be kept alive among young Malay Singaporeans in the face of the community's increasing adaptation and growing use of English. Going forward, the importance of the national language must be reflected in the community as that of the original inhabitants of Singapore — the *pribumi or bumiputra* (literally means "sons of the soil/land"). Malay Singaporeans must see the use of the national language as their contribution to the growth of a multiethnic Singaporean Singapore. I see no contradiction in this — the more Malay is used as the national language, the more Singaporean we become. As the "sons of the soil", the Malays are also the living reminder of Singapore's glorious past centuries ago as a trading post, much like today, when Malay was the regional *lingua franca.* The revival of the national language as the glue for a 21st century Singapore provides the continuity amid change that PM Lee so vividly talked about. Just as crucial, it is a fitting and timely tribute to the legacy of modern Singapore's founding PM, Lee Kuan Yew.

Chapter 10

The Hub Concept — Reflections on the Past, Projections for the Future*

Joergen Oerstroem Moeller

---

*This article was originally published in Commentary, Volume 24 titled "Singapore @ 50: Reflections and Observations" © 2015 The National University of Singapore Society. Professor Joergen Oerstroem Moeller was Visiting Senior Research Fellow at the Institute of Southeast Asian Studies at the time of writing, which is now renamed ISEAS – Yusof Ishak Institute.

Over the preceding fifty years, Singapore has earned the right and honour of being labelled the number one hub in the world — absolute leader, uncontested and indisputable.

In the prism of today, it seems obvious, almost self-evident, but this was far from the case when Singapore started to look for a way forward after Independence in 1965. Most of the arguments against success — small population, small economy, and a small market — were turned on their head to become assets by plugging into the role of being a hub.

It would not have been possible without reading and interpreting the geopolitical and geo-economic development trends correctly. In 1965, the world was divided, broadly speaking, between a capitalist group of countries then led by the United States (US), a socialist part spearheaded by the Soviet Union, and the so-called Third World or non-aligned group. Many analysts burnt their fingers and looked back at prognoses with trepidation in case somebody remembered! I have just recalled that around 1950, the prevailing mood was that the "winners" in Asia would be the Philippines, Vietnam and Burma as it was then known — this is completely wrong! The forecasts and evaluations overlooked the fact that it was not resource-rich economies that would get the upper hand, but instead, it was countries that were able to assume control over their own destiny and realise where they could find and exploit a comparative advantage. Singapore did so through the hub concept, just as China did so with Deng Xiaoping's reforms.

This tells us that good governance, the ability to read future trends correctly and even more crucially, the will to take advantage of those trends that vastly overshadows the level of natural endowment — resources.

It also tells us that political leaders must master the ability to communicate with the population on the course of development which is being set and the reason for it. Otherwise, a nation cannot rally the majority of people behind the chosen policy.

Political leaders must have the ability to adjust and adapt all the time. What is good today may not be so tomorrow. The first mover advantage is crucial when adopting the hub concept amongst other things because success demands infrastructure investments often at so large a scale that it becomes impossible for it to be changed or discontinued without large costs incurred. Mistakes cannot be remedied with just a snap of the fingers.

While it might seem easier for Singapore to be as adroit and nimble as it has been than larger countries, this does not distract from the achievements of those who saw what was coming and made the country ready. There is an old saying that opportunities come to those who are ready for them — and in this respect, Singapore scores well.

The first step was, as has almost always been the case, to start with labour-intensive and low-cost manufacturing. Apparel is the classic example — it also worked for Singapore, but only for a limited time.

The next step was to exploit the geography by building harbour facilities. If the British Empire saw Singapore's geography as an asset and built a naval base, then the same would probably be true for shipping. Transport to and from Singapore is very limited, in view of the small Singapore market. However, a harbour serving as a hub for transport in-and-out of the region promised a larger market.

Singapore may have been lucky in the sense that the global supply chain built around outsourcing and offshoring took off in the 1980s giving harbour facilities of this kind — transhipment — a phenomenal boost, but the crucial observation is that this could have been done by everybody in Southeast Asia, but was only done successfully by Singapore. First mover advantage paid off handsomely as the competitors took time to build facilities. This enabled Singapore to shape a good relationship with the big shipping liners and container transporters whilst gaining experience in handling this apparently simple operation, but which is in fact rather sophisticated if it is to achieve cost effectiveness also.

The same can be said about Changi Airport and Singapore Airlines. In fact very few would have dared to predict the success of these two cornerstones of Singapore's economy. There is no reason why Singapore should get this big slice of the cake, outmaneuvering other countries, cities, or airports within the region with a larger domestic market, except of course, that Singapore spotted the opportunity first before anybody else — first mover advantage.

All the endeavours and activities to build an industry around Information and Communication Technology (ICT) brought Singapore the distinction of being among the top of the group of ICT countries in the world. This is good in itself, but more important is the spinoff effect of reducing costs and enhancing opportunities for doing business, making it attractive for international firms to set up regional or even global headquarters in Singapore.

The whole idea of good governance around effective and efficient administration has underlined Singapore's role as the place where, by far, most international companies come to set up headquarters, research or financial centres. This produces another spin off effect of drawing talented people to Singapore, enhancing the intellectual capital of the nation.

This so-called first phase of the hub was moulded around traditional economic and industrial sectors. What is not always incorporated in analyses is that Singapore aspired to be a global player albeit in select and narrow sectors. At the same time, it worked towards being identified as an island of efficiency, good governance, integrity and where rule of law prevailed.

The next step of development was focused on building up the services sector. This was more difficult to do and the risks were higher, but the branding as a place for good governance helped.

Singapore is a key global financial hub today. The difficulty was and still is about the ability to strike the right balance: Being a successful financial hub requires effective facilities and good governance. If uncertainty starts to reign, money and subsequently the financial service sector will move. The costs of doing so are bearable for the large financial institutions. The international efforts in gaining ground to combat money laundering and obscure financial transactions, including harbouring dubious person's and/or organisations' money, forces a financial hub such as Singapore to act according not only to international rules, but also to moral and political guidelines. Unless one can see what is in the pipeline, there is a risk of being caught and placed under suspicion. Being a hub for global money embeds fragility and vulnerability — few things can move faster than money. For Singapore, that implies the need for continuous, high quality vigilance and not misjudging legal and moral boundaries of what is permissible.

The hub concept has also been applied to healthcare and education sectors. The interesting aspect is cost and quality weighed against each other. People going for an operation will do this calculation as will those sending their children for education. Singapore is at the higher end of the market and that is good. However, the challenge is to make sure that the higher prices are matched by higher quality.

Leisure and culture have joined the list. The Esplanade (nicknamed "the Durian") has since signalled a new approach, which has been reinforced with the development of the two integrated resorts. Singapore tapped into the vast flow of money in the slipstream of tourism, namely entertainment such as Formula One and gambling. The latter was a controversial policy to adopt. The integrated resorts with their casinos posed the same dilemma as the financial sector, but in a much harder manner — a balance had to be struck. How do we ensure that procedures and controls are able to prevent a dent in Singapore's image as a low crime country? In a way, Singapore acquiesced to a low key rebranding to become less "boring" and more "adventurous". This decision illustrates the dilemma sometimes associated with the hub concept. Singapore could have said "no" to the casinos, but the consequence would not only have been to forego this kind of business, but also to see other entertainment and leisure activities go elsewhere — a potential negative spinoff.

The main lessons gathered, so far, can be summarised in this way: Governance and foresight are the ultimate and indispensable conditions for achieving a hub status for any activity.

The hubs stemming from the first and second wave of development in Singapore have considerable mileage, but it cannot be denied that they are on the downward trajectory and have to be supplemented by what is termed a third wave. What then are the opportunities to look out for?

The global supply chain is going to be replaced by regional supply chains. Singapore can take advantage of the trend where the region is beginning to shape its own economy and need no longer be held hostage to the fortunes of the US or European economy. Figures for intra-trade (trade among a group of countries) as a share of total trade reveals that 55 percent of the trade among East Asian countries is intra-regional, compared to 64 percent for the European Union (EU) and 45 percent for The North American Free Trade Agreement (NAFTA).

McKinsey Global Institute suggests that Southeast Asia can benefit from this development in three ways:

> Firstly, successful implementation of the ASEAN Economic Community integration plan could significantly increase trade and create a single market of 600 million consumers. Secondly, ASEAN can expand its free-trade agreements and attract additional production from multinationals as labor costs in China continue to rise. Together, these opportunities could create some $280 billion to $625 billion a year in economic value by 2030. To realise this potential, ASEAN will need to tackle restrictions on foreign investment, to develop a more competitive manufacturing sector, and to build critical foundations, such as infrastructure, logistics, and workforce skills.

This trend will strengthen over the coming decades. Production for consumption within the East Asian region could possibly overtake that for exports. It will also be the same for South Asia, although this may take a little more time. Prime Minister Narendra Modi of India has tabled an economic policy that is similar to that pursued by East Asian countries, moving them away from labour-intensive, low-cost manufacturing activities to higher value-add ones.

Singapore will be, enviably, well-situated to exploit these new trade patterns. It may require some new infrastructure as containerships for regional transport that may be different in size from those built for global transport and the trade in resources such as bulk shipping, may not go through Singapore. However, that might only dent and not remove the opportunities.

A massive restructuring of global trade is under way for energy. Watching the world's energy supply and demand, a number of factors work against global transport. Shale gas and oil have been discovered in all major industrial countries except in Japan. Self-sufficiency is in vogue for strategic and geopolitical reasons. Oil may give way to coal and LNG (liquefied natural gas). Exploitation of the hub's opportunities asks for a correct reading of these new patterns and will undoubtedly require investments in infrastructure to be in place to tap those opportunities.

Broadly speaking, global trade over the last fifty years have been steered by an East-West axis — a supply chain with production in Asia and consumption in the US and the EU, supplemented by transport of resources along the same axis with some, but minor exceptions.

The axis runs from China, over South Asia and on to Africa. Every year, these three geographical areas account for an increasing share of the world's population, the lion's share of global growth, a higher share of global income, and a rising purchasing power.

It is too early to sketch a final model, but it would look somewhat like this: China will transfer labour-intensive and low-cost manufacturing to some countries in Southeast Asia (Vietnam, Indonesia and maybe Myanmar), but primarily to Bangladesh which has already benefitted. The same goes for Pakistan as well as India which is coming up even faster if Prime Minister Modi's policy succeeds. The substitute for labour-intensive and low-cost manufacturing in China will be higher value-added production competing on quality, service, technology, and branding. Africa will, for the first decade or two, step into the role of the supplier of resources (energy and raw material), but as time goes by, its rising labour force combined with the effect of high growth will attract manufacturing investments.

Approaching 2050, it is likely, almost certain, that labour-intensive manufacturing will have completed its transfer from China to South Asia, and be on its way to Africa. People have long spoken about China as an economic powerhouse, but China's rise will be nothing compared to the axis of China-South Asia-Africa.

For Singapore, this is mixed news. Geographically, it will find itself on the fringe of the new power axis. The challenge is, however, more for Southeast Asia as a whole. The region is economically too small to serve as a viable platform for economic growth. It not only strengthens the well-known arguments to plug into the Chinese and Japanese markets, but adds a new dimension which is the ability to be part of the new growth scenario. If Southeast Asia can do that, and omens are looking good with economic and industrial structure, the region may benefit and Singapore, as a hub in Southeast Asia and part of the East Asian supply chain, may fare even better than what the global supply chain offered.

The industrial age is coming to an end — economic and industrial structures built according to the needs of that age are becoming obsolete. The coming age will be shaped by scarcities. The world can already feel the effects of food shortages, rising resource prices combined with physical scarcities for some resources, an energy problem, water scarcity for almost half of global population, and clean environment as something which cannot be taken for granted.

It is a safe bet that those cities and countries, knowing how to use resources efficiently, recycling resources and moving into remanufacturing and a number of other measures to reduce resource use will be the eventual winners. Many policies to this effect can be implemented. One of them is the shifting emphasis to research, technology, innovation, and invention, from the saving of manpower, which steered the innovation process throughout the industrial age, to the saving of resources.

For a small and nimble society such as Singapore, this can be done and the city-state has it within its grasp, the ability to position itself as a hub for application of the new paradigm which controls production and consumption.

Urbanisation may well be one of the most important issues in the decades to come and focus will be on sustainable cities, liveable cities, and cities which manage to save resources. What can be better for Singapore than taking the lead here?

Above this comes an offer Singapore cannot refuse! Most societies around the world are unfortunately, becoming more violent, making people feel insecure. There is a growing demand for human security in a broader sense — the ability to be able to walk safely on the streets, no fear of robbery, and no worries for children's safety — essentially, a safe haven for human beings. Those who look for such a place are usually well-off. Strengthening its image, and it will be easy as a quality society, Singapore will attract such people. It fits in very nicely with the trends sketched above as a third-generation hub.

Taken together, the futuristic view of the next fifty years suggests that the hub concept is likely to be very much alive. It only requires the same adroitness and ability to adjust and adapt as seen already over the first fifty years. Governance, boldness, and a correct reading of future trends are called for. It is not easy, but indispensable for Singapore if it wishes to maintain its hard-won place as one of the best societies in the world.

Society

Chapter 11

Social Participation in a New Singapore*

Ho Kong Chong, Hasliza Ahmad, Helen Sim and Ho Zhi Wei

*This article was originally published in Commentary, Volume 24 titled "Singapore @ 50: Reflections and Observations" © 2015 The National University of Singapore Society. Dr Ho Kong Chong is an Associate Professor of Sociology at the Faculty of Arts and Social Sciences, National University of Singapore. Hasliza Ahmad, Helen Sim, and Ho Zhi Wei were officers from the Research & Planning Division at the National Youth Council, Singapore.

Introduction

Our youths are witnessing dramatic changes to Singapore's social landscape. For instance, while almost nine in 10 persons in Singapore were citizens in the 1990s, this declined to six in 10 by 2014.[1] As Singapore's population continues to grow through immigration, the population in the Republic will become more heterogeneous as new citizens and permanent residents bring their established ways of doing things, along with different social and cultural norms.

This greater level of heterogeneity presents a social integration challenge for hosts and new residents alike. With the small size and high density living of Singapore, the resultant increase in population density through immigration brings people of different social backgrounds physically closer. Thus, in everyday life, congestion (in the use of social and public services) and competition (in school and work) may create greater potential for misunderstanding and conflict. Everyday examples where there is a clash of cultural norms and habitual behaviour are in the practices of queuing, maintaining physical distance in crowded situations, tones of speech in public places, forms of courtesy towards fellow users, etc.

If we were to accept the argument that Singapore is a global city and a small city-state where the mobility and immigration of people (i.e., service professionals, industry workers and domestic helpers, tourists, and students as well) are necessary for the economy, then it is just as necessary for Singapore society to embrace temporary visitors, permanent residents, and new citizens. Herein lies the importance of cultivating a deeper appreciation and understanding among different social and ethnic groups while fostering greater social cohesion in Singapore.

[1] Department of Statistics, *Population Trends 2014* (Singapore: Department of Statistics, 2014), http://www.singstat.gov.sg/publications/publications_and_papers/population_and_population_structure/population2014.pdf, v.

Diversity, Friendships, and Singapore's Youths

Singapore's increasing diversity and heterogeneity have been most keenly felt by our youths, given that the resident youth population has not kept pace with the growth of the overall population. While one in three persons was a resident youth in the 1990s, this proportion has since declined to one in five persons by 2014.[2] As social diversity increases, there is a tendency for trust to erode within and across ethnic groups in the short-to-medium term, particularly if there is a lack of frequent, socially diverse interaction.[3] Considering the multiethnic nature of Singapore society, it is vital that youths develop deeper and meaningful friendships that span multiple social groups and communities to maintain trust and social cohesion.

Drawing from the National Youth Survey (NYS) 2013, a number of patterns may be observed attesting to the value of friendship diversity in maintaining trust and social cohesion within and across ethnic groups. When asked whether they were comfortable with someone of a different race being their neighbour, we found that youths with close friends of a different race reported greater levels of comfort, a mean of 4.53 on a 5-point scale with 5 being "strongly agree". In contrast, youths without close friends of a different race reported a lower mean of 4.24. The differences are even greater when it comes to neighbourly relations. Youths with close friends of a different nationality reported greater comfort with someone of a different nationality who is a neighbour with a mean of 4.29; while

---

[2] Department of Statistics, *Census of Population 2000* (Singapore: Department of Statistics, 2000), http://www.singstat.gov.sg/Publications/publications_and_papers/cop2000/census_2000_release1/excel/t1-7.xls; Department of Statistics, *Population Trends 2014*.

[3] Putnam, Robert D., "E pluribusunum: Diversity and community in the twenty-first century," *Scandinavian Political Studies* 30, no. 2 (2007): 137–174; Stolle, Dietlind, Soroka, Stuart, and Johnston, Richard, "When does diversity erode trust? Neighborhood diversity, interpersonal trust and the mediating effect of social interactions," *Political Studies* 56, no. 1 (2008): 57–75.

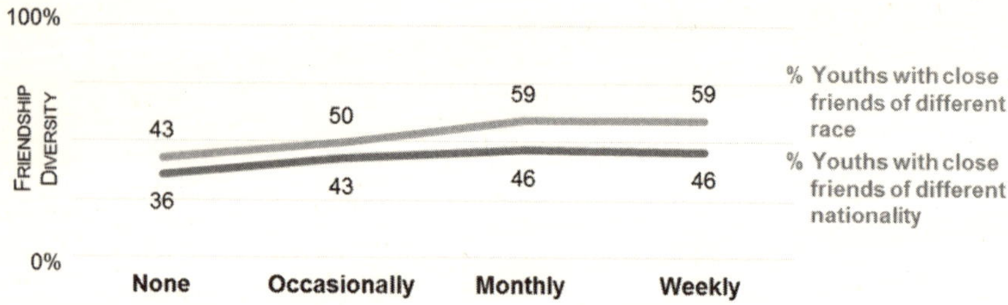

Figure 1: Friendship Diversity and Participation Frequency

Source: National Youth Survey (NYS), 2013.

youths without close friends of a different nationality reported a mean of 3.91.

From a policy perspective, we think that social participation among youths can shape their friendship patterns and through these networks, create an acceptance of diverse ethnicities and nationalities. Indeed, based on the available data from NYS 2013, we found this positive correlation between friendship diversity and social participation. Figure 1 illustrates the correlation between friendship diversity and frequency of youths' social participation. Our measure of social participation includes activities in a variety of domains such as arts & culture, sports, uniformed groups, community and welfare programmes, religion, and workplace.

For inter-ethnic relationships, there is a big jump of 7 percent between non-participants and occasional participants, and another 9 percent jump from occasional to regular participation. Inter-nationality relations show a 7 percent increase between non-participants and those with occasional participation, moderating at 46 percent for regular participation — there was no difference between monthly and weekly participation in friendship diversity for race and nationality.

Taken together, the survey data suggests that enhancing social participation of youths through the establishment of more diverse friendships and connecting youths with different population segments may be a way to build a more cohesive society.

Benefiting from Social Participation

Beyond friendship diversity, there are other benefits that youths can derive from social participation that will be valuable to thriving and maintaining social cohesion in a rapidly changing and diversifying society. Table 1 provides a summary of these benefits in terms of multicultural orientation, interpersonal relationships, outward orientation, and civic engagement.

With the exception of the last item in Table 1, the indicators presented are attitudinal and reflect the degree to which the survey

Table 1: Benefits of social participation among youths

	Not Involved in Any Group	Active in at Least One Group	Difference
Multicultural Orientation			
Respect values and beliefs of other groups	81%	86%	5%
Knowledgeable about people of other races	39%	50%	11%
Interpersonal Relationships			
Caring about other people's feelings	80%	83%	3%
Good at making friends	55%	64%	9%
Working well with others	69%	75%	6%
Leading a team of people	43%	56%	13%
Outward Orientation			
Public speaking	20%	34%	14%
Adapting to change	63%	72%	9%
Civic Engagement			
To be actively involved in local volunteer work	7%	15%	8%
To be actively involved in overseas volunteer work	5%	11%	6%
Worked with fellow citizens to solve a problem in your community	1%	8%	7%

Source: National Youth Survey (NYS), 2013.

participants agree with these statements about themselves. The differences between the involved and uninvolved for the volunteering items is 8 percent in relation to local volunteering and 6 percent in relation to overseas volunteering suggest that involvement in social groups is associated (though not necessarily causal in nature) with volunteerism. This is clearly important for society as, the care of the weak and vulnerable are within the voluntary sector. Another form of civic engagement is community participation. This item is particularly important because it is a behavioural measure, indicating that respondents actually worked to solve a community problem. For this item, the difference between involved and non-involved youths is a significant 7 percent.

The other socially important goal is our multicultural orientation. Singapore's growing social diversity makes it more important that we adopt a multicultural orientation. Table 1 indicates that there are significantly higher percentages posted by involved youths with regard to respect for the values and beliefs of other groups (5 percent difference) and the knowledge about people of other races (11 percent difference). Indeed, most social groups that have an open membership criteria, and those which are larger in size, have within these groups, social diversity in terms of religion and ethnicity and to a certain extent, nationality. Membership in such groupings requires individuals to learn about, accommodate, and embrace such differences.

Besides the socially important goals of volunteering and multicultural orientations, participation in groups is also associated with a set of important interpersonal skills: public speaking (14 percent difference), leadership (13 percent difference), making friends (9 percent difference), adapting to change (9 percent difference), working well with others (6 percent difference), and caring about the feelings of others (3 percent difference). The important point to take away from this set of interpersonal skills is that these cannot really be taught within the classroom. Therefore, to the extent that these are learnt interpersonally and within the everyday routines of group activities, social participation then provides an essential function of preparing individuals to adapt effectively to multicultural living.

Cultivating Social Participation

Participation in social groups brings unintended benefits to the individual and society. Young people join social groups such as sports, arts and cultural, and hobby groups for the immediate benefit of fulfilling their interests but in the course of doing so, they also learn new skills necessary for the promotion of such interests as well as values necessary for teamwork to occur.

Perhaps more importantly, such group-derived attributes benefit society, as friendship diversity and multicultural attitudes acquired through social participation help to foster integration in society. It is significant to note that these attributes play a sustained and important role in everyday life. Individuals with friendship diversity and multicultural attitudes are the brokers or bridges in different communities which foster a better understanding of social differences. While organisations can only work in prescribed settings, such individuals in significant numbers and from different socio-economic backgrounds are able to socially navigate society more easily. Within social groups, interactions are regular and sustained. The diverse friendships that arise from such contexts are more intimate and multicultural attitudes formed in such settings and at a young age are strongly held.

If such behaviour cannot be taught in the classroom and can only be learnt within the context of social groups, then there is a renewed role for youths to participate in groups to create such orientations. The overriding focus cannot be on integration alone, because this naked goal can never be the binding agent between individuals. Instead, the focus has to be on a set of activities that draw youths of similar interests together, such as sports, arts and culture, hobby groups, and so on. Common interests will sustain diverse friendships — multicultural orientation can only be a by-product albeit an important one.

Social Participation and a New National Youth Council

The National Youth Council (NYC) was formed in 1989 as the national coordinating body for youth affairs to support youth aspirations, to enable them to lead purposeful, robust, and balanced lives, and help them contribute positively to the nation. Twenty-five years on, NYC remains committed to the goal of supporting youth aspirations and action for the community. Yet, our society has undergone significant change, and this prompts thoughtful reflection on the role of NYC today.

Our youth social landscape has changed with the Republic's ascendance as a global city. Singapore is global city, nation, and home. Embedded within a global city, Singapore's youths are diverse, innovative, and expressive. They are also highly connected to non-traditional sources of information and opinion. As young citizens, our youths also feel the strain of living in a global city. Growing social heterogeneity and stratification, increased competition, and living costs have compounded the challenges youths face today. There exists an urgent need to ensure our youths possess the resilience to meet these challenges, and in particular, develop trust across ethnic and socio-economic lines.

Given these emergent needs, it is timely that NYC was restructured in 2015 to expand its focus on developing social participation among youths today. Already, a good proportion of youths desire to contribute to society, with some setting up social enterprises and non-profit organisations.[4] Compared to just a handful when NYC was founded, there are over 200 active non-government affiliated youth sector organisations (YSOs) today. With Outward Bound Singapore and Youth Corps Singapore now part of the new autonomous agency under the Ministry of Culture, Community and Youth (MCCY), the new NYC is poised to prepare youths for new challenges and empower them to shape their future.

---

[4]The National Youth Survey 2013 found a good proportion of youths regard "helping the less fortunate" (41 percent) and "contributing back to society" (39 percent) as "very important" life goals in their lives.

Examples of NYC programmes that will benefit from this transition are the Youth Expedition Project and the recently formed Youth Corps Singapore. These programmes bring diverse individuals together in their formative years regardless of cultural, socio-economic, or academic backgrounds to meet and solve community needs. Involvement in such programmes often creates the beginnings of a new awareness in young people:

> Most of us tend to dismiss troubled youths as just being rebellious. However, after interacting with the local beneficiaries, I learnt that there are a lot of social factors that contribute to their state of affairs, such as family background and lack of opportunities. [...] As different as we are based on race, culture, and upbringing, ultimately, we all aspire towards the same goals and aspirations in life.
>
> Youth Expedition Project Participant, Project Diya V, 2014

> This journey hasn't been easy with a lot of time and effort spent, and sacrifices. However, it has revealed the resilience and determination in me. [...] I made new discoveries about myself through engaging the community, understanding the importance of listening, and changing and opening up new perspectives in the way I view and define things, such as success.
>
> Youth Corps Singapore Participant, Cohort 1, 2014

By expanding these initiatives, the new NYC hopes to bridge youths across social strata to foster meaningful relationships and mutual understanding necessary for social cohesion. These national-level initiatives also offer opportunities for our young people to develop the necessary tenacity and resilience to meet challenges in life. The life skills training and mentoring which participants receive aims to help our youths navigate an increasingly diverse and complex society. This is part of the new NYC 's vision — to develop our youths to be discerning, resilient, and active citizens.

As NYC builds up its capacity, plans are in place to increase ground-up initiatives and mentorship programmes. Through the National Youth Fund, YSOs can expect a larger pool of funds to support their social initiatives for youths, and youths can expect that there will be mentors to guide their local projects or personal development. As youths leave formal education, youth-led initiatives will play a particularly valuable role in providing further opportunities for them to benefit from social participation, and enable subsequent generations of youths to do so.

Conclusion

More than a decade ago, then-Prime Minister Goh Chok Tong articulated his vision of a global city and anticipated the need and challenges of building a strong social compact as he rounded off his 2001 National Day Rally, "Remaking Singapore":

> For our growth strategy and social compact to be effective, Singapore must be cohesive as a nation. [...] If we have the courage to confront problems instead of skirting them, if we are prepared to endure temporary hardships, and if we can adapt to change, we can continue to do better. This New Singapore — a global city with a strong social compact — is the Mount Everest we must achieve. We must succeed, so that our children can face tomorrow with optimism and confidence.[5]

Today, the need for a strong social compact in a highly globalised Singapore remains ever more relevant. It is like scaling Mount Everest because Singapore is both an emergent global city and a young nation. Data from the NYS suggests that enhancing the social participation of youths may be the way forward. Having more young people with diverse friendships and stronger multicultural orientations could help foster a better understanding of social differences in society and broker or bridge differences across

[5] Goh, Chok Tong, speech in English by the Prime Minister in his National Day Rally Address, National Cultural Centre, National University of Singapore, August 19, 2001, http://www.nas.gov.sg/archivesonline/speeches/view-html?filename=2001081903.htm.

communities. To do this, the new NYC will need to leverage on collaborations with public and private sector organisations. Through these efforts, we can equip our youths to surmount the challenges of a global city; seize opportunities to fulfil their dreams and aspirations; and contribute to building and shaping the future of Singapore.

Chapter 12

Singapore 100: Becoming a City of Good*

Melissa Kwee

*This article was originally published in Commentary, Volume 25 titled "A Democracy of Deeds and Problem Solving" © 2016 The National University of Singapore Society. Melissa Kwee was the Chief Executive Officer of the National Volunteer & Philanthropy Centre.

> Why should we be in such desperate haste to succeed, and in such desperate enterprises? If a man does not keep pace with his companions, perhaps it is because he hears a different drummer. Let him step to the music which he hears, however measured or far away.[1]

> Do not think that I have come to destroy the Law or the Prophets. I did not come to destroy but to fulfil.[2]

At the cusp of our next fifty years as an independent city-state, we stand in a Singapore challenged by rising economic pressures, shifting demographic trends and conflicting ideologies that keep both the policy circles and coffee shops buzzing with discussion about that future. However, Singapore has emerged from SG50 — code for Singapore at its 50 years of Independence — stronger, clearer and more united about who we are and what kind of a country we want to build.

There is a new *zeitgeist* brewing, as seen in a rise in local pride around our built, natural and cultural heritage that has, in turn, made cookbooks, local hipster cafes and all manner of tourist paraphernalia rise in popularity. Local icons of culture are being celebrated, reinterpreted and revived. For the youth, it is suddenly "cool" to be Singaporean. For our senior citizens who lived through the early years of Independence, we honoured them with accolades of leadership and hefty Pioneer Generation packages. The rest of us are mostly glad we live in a clean, safe and efficient country where the laws and other rules of governance are clear, recognised and enforced (even if there are too many of them).

During the Jubilee celebrations of 2015, we stopped all of our busyness and took note of those around us who are in greater social need, such as the elderly, people with disability, and the poor and disadvantaged families. We set aside our differences to be grateful about what we have and reflected on how we achieved that. Our differences did not disappear, the economic outlook did not become

---

[1] Thoreau, Henry David, *Walden* (Boston, MA: Ticknor and Fields).

[2] Gospel of Matthew 5:17.

more favourable and manna did not descend from heaven, so to speak. However, I observed, that we had become a Singapore that was comfortable with candid conversations about what has worked and what has not in bringing about socio-economic progress. There was humility in that conversation. There was even a shift in certain perspectives about what it means to live the good life or indeed, what it means to be the "Singaporean of the Year".

The Straits Times Singaporean of the Year 2015 awardee, the first ever, Ms Noriza Mansor, aged 50, was not a technopreneur, a business tycoon, or a President's Scholar. Ms Mansor is a bedsheet promoter who works in department stores selling various brands of mass-market linens. You would have forgotten about her if not for an action that the peer judges believed embodied what is best about being Singaporean.

Noriza was celebrated because she had washed and cared for an elderly man who had soiled himself in a public square as he ran an errand with his wife who was in a wheelchair. Why did the good Samaritan story trump the stories of personal bests that other potential awardees were feted for? What was it that spoke to her peers and judges?

I imagine it was that Ms Mansor, with her quiet and practical problem-resolution abilities, embodied what we do best: we do not make a lot of fuss when there is a problem. Instead, we get to the root of the issue and attempt to solve it as efficiently and effectively as possible. Except in this instance, this was not a business or policy concern; it was instead a human issue and was addressed in a way that restored human dignity.

Despite being technocratic and practical, Singaporeans intuitively know what is best about being Singaporean and about being human: giving and receiving, loving and being loved, being productive and enjoying meaningful fruits of our labour.

Looking ahead to SG100, it is timely to reflect on the meaning of "success", to give thanks for the origins of that success and ask: For what purpose is it that we have succeeded? Beyond reflecting on the transformation from slum to shimmering metropolis or the relevance of the 5Cs (condominium, credit card, car, cash and country club membership), fundamental questions about our collective purpose and identity as a nation, are percolating. Do we have a soul or are we simply highly functional pragmatists? Is Singapore a city of good? Do people define the good life as a grateful and giving life, or is it defined by just having several good things? This is a conversation that is just beginning.

Who are the people who are trying to make sense of this and are forging new practices and identities? What issues and circumstances have brought about these opportunities to develop those practices and identities? What patterns do we observe that can be strengthened to share the fruits of our success?

This essay seeks to explore five trends that define this new spirit of Singapore through the lens of civic action and community-building: skills-based volunteering; youth volunteering; businesses partnering each other to do good; family-based community initiatives; and informal, community-based giving. Finally, it concludes with some practical ideas to build on these.

Skills-based Volunteering: Because We All Have a Skill to Offer

Today, being a professional is more than just about doing a job. More millennials are interviewing companies to see if they are the kind of company they want to work for. As uncomfortable as it may feel, this is the new reality — employees want more out of employment than just a job. For example, the pro-bono initiative of the Law Society of Singapore is driven by passionate young lawyers whose thirst for justice have not been met in their day jobs. Another example is how Chartered Financial Analyst (CFA) Australia and a number of the "Big Four" accounting firms are seeking to institutionally support charities with pro bono hours and services. A third example is the trend of medical and nursing students who are seeking projects locally and regionally to exercise their skills and address real needs around us. A fourth example that comes to mind is an initiative by the School of Chemical and Life Sciences (CLS) Optometry department at Singapore Polytechnic that organises eye examinations in Cambodia on a regular basis. It also collects disused spectacles in Singapore, catalogues them and distributes them to villagers in Cambodia.

Beyond the traditional professions, we see hairdressers offering haircuts to the elderly poor or those who are bedridden. "I feel so humbled when I see people line up just so I can cut their hair," remarked a neighbourhood hairdresser involved in such an initiative.

We all have skills and this is part of a more holistic "SkillsFuture" programme, if it is possible to borrow the name of the government skills development scheme. The programmes above allow for the honing of skills while there is also the creation of social value.

Youth Volunteering: Because We Learn to Identify Needs and Address Them

Skills volunteering is also changing youth volunteering. Most people volunteer in their youth, but sustaining volunteering into their adult lives has been the challenge. Initiatives are now shifting to focus on meaning-making, empowering youth with skills to understand needs rather than simply robotically implementing programmes, and connecting them to communities of purpose and practice instead, in this second new trend in giving and doing good in Singapore.

Modelled after the best of national youth initiatives, Youth Corps Singapore is raising the game at the national level. It is bringing the spirit of service to youth by offering them a way to serve, learn and develop life-long friendships in a fellowship built on a common commitment to serve. Perhaps over time, we will see more of the best and brightest use their talents to serve society. For instance, why not establish the equivalent of the "Teach for America" model in Singapore which reaches people in the Southeast Asian region? Fundamental to effective youth volunteering is a service learning methodology where the youth adopt critical life skills which include needs assessment, reflection and meaning-making, and community collaboration that will also serve them well and keep them engaged in such work later in life.

Business for Good: Because Partnering Others Creates Greater Impact

A third trend in this new spirit of service is found in how businesses analyse, design and execute community initiatives. Corporate social responsibility, while not new in Singapore, is taking on new forms where leaders are not just doing their "day of service" or presenting cheques, but creating platforms and mobilising others to multiply their impact.

IBM initiated one such effort amongst businesses in their neighbourhood at the Changi Business Park. Instead of being an exclusively IBM initiative, they organised "Changi Business Park Gives" as a platform to engage businesses in the area and provide an opportunity to work with the South West Community Development Council on identifying neighbourhood needs that businesses could address with skilled volunteers, funds, and meaningful collaboration. The result? An impressive 90,000 hours committed by employees and donations of over $85,000. The benefit of size, an IBM leader told me, was to leverage it to serve others. She expressed great pride that their efforts enabled smaller businesses in the neighbourhood to get a taste of volunteering and community work by working with more experienced volunteers.

However, large multinationals are not the only ones organising platforms and coalitions to do good. The local food enterprise, Samsui Supplies & Services, the subsidiary of the Soup Restaurant Group, wanted to do something to care for the nutrition of the elderly. For their 2014 #GivingTuesday, a national day of giving, Samsui pledged to serve 30,000 quality meals to the elderly in nursing homes, daycare centres and other community facilities. To fulfil this pledge, they partnered their suppliers to contribute ingredients, logistics support and donations.

Director of Samsui Supplies & Services, Ang Kian Peng was inspired by a mentor who believed that giving was part of doing good business. "He taught me that we should help others with what we do best. We are in the food business, so we want to help those who cannot afford decent meals on a daily basis," Ang said. Other than the impact on the elderly through the programme, Kian Peng 's greatest satisfaction was in bringing together many people from different walks of life to form friendships that have been deeply fulfilling.

Family-based Giving: Because We Learn What We Live

As families get smaller and where there is more intentional parenting, we also see the initial seedlings of family-based giving emerge in a fourth trend. This practice teaches values of gratitude and sharing, strengthens family ties, promotes a sense of self-efficacy and the belief that we can bring about positive change to the world around us.

At the National Volunteer & Philanthropy Centre (NVPC), we know that the small and simple ideas work best. Last year, during Chinese New Year, we seeded the idea of giving *hongbaos* to the poor by featuring a story of two brothers who decided to donate part of their *hongbao* money to a charity whose cause was meaningful to their family. Through a collaboration with the Singapore Kindness Movement and the dailies, the story generated a 73 percent year-on-year increase in donations to charities that month. Small idea — big difference. Most of all, it changed families' approach to giving by inviting them to think about who to give to and the reason for it.

To share a more personal anecdote about this, my family has added a visit to a block of one-room flats to our Chinese New Year tradition. We host a dessert party for the children at their void deck. We also visit the elderly staying in the block with oranges and have conversations with them. We did these for the first time last year, and more friends and family joined in this year. At the end of it, my cousin even asked me whether we could go back regularly, outside of the Chinese New Year season.

Informal and Community-based Giving: Because Everyone Can Do Something

A challenge most agencies involved in volunteering grapple with is the misalignment between the service offered and the type of charity. This includes the need to cater to after-office hours, bite-size projects; training requirements; training courses offered only a few times a year to get volunteers ready; and a misunderstanding of what precisely is needed by charities that want support from volunteers.

This difficulty in alignment has given rise to new outlets in community-based and informal giving where passionate neighbours have disintermediated charities by analysing issues at the ground level and creating their own solutions rather than doing these through existing charities. This is the fifth trend in the emerging spirit of giving in Singapore.

To illustrate what I mean, let me cite the "Learning Friends", "Early Reader" and "Keeping Hope Alive" programmes. Children whose parents are in jail are often disadvantaged. A group of friends created a training programme and deployed student and adult befrienders to visit the homes of such children to become their "Learning Friends". Their mission is to build the children's sense of self-confidence and worth.

"Early Reader" has been running for over a year and has developed both corporate and institutional partnerships with companies and tertiary students who are now trained, prepared and supported to read to their "early reader friends".

"Keeping Hope Alive" emerged organically based on a "first responder" concept that organises volunteers to visit elderly folks living alone and other one-room Housing and Development Board (HDB) residents. The volunteers assess and address the needs. They fix cupboards, buy new mattresses, cut nails, raise funds for surgery and help the residents get connected to the variety of services available which are not always accessible to them. The organiser invites volunteers to do this every Saturday morning. With more people, she says, they can go deeper and further to keep the sense of hope alive among the elderly and residents of one-room flats. What makes them different is their attitude — they feel blessed by the opportunity to serve. They are a new type of volunteer group that recognises that it is they who are beneficiaries, and those whom they serve, their teachers.

"Sayang Kalimantan" went further afield to make a difference. It sought to tackle the haze in Kalimantan. In the midst of us choking from the haze here in Singapore, the founders asked themselves what it must be like for those living at the source of the haze and decided to render help there. The protagonist was a videographer who went to Kalimantan to offer masks and commercial grade air purifiers which were crowdfunded online to residents there and to tell their story. He is now trying to adopt that particular village and offer more regular support by way of training to create "clean air safe houses" which can be set up when the burning starts again. He is trying to develop alternative livelihoods for the villagers. This might sound like just a drop in the ocean, but as a drop in that village, he is an ocean of goodwill.

Imagining the Possibilities of Making a Difference

What do these initiatives and projects have in common? How can they be amplified?

They all begin with a certain imagination of what is possible. There is a story that provokes, captivates and mobilises the will to take action. We need to tell more stories about how this can happen.

However, stories and inspiration where no outlet exists to do good could result in cruel frustration and in what some call "slacktivism". We know that a simple "like" or "tweet" does not fundamentally change things or result in successful action. Anecdotes can describe a need but they cannot result in fundamental change. We need ground-level enquiry and patience to understand the real issues to make headway.

That understanding then has to be connected to possibilities and resources for action. People and groups will have to struggle to define the real needs and create platforms for themselves and others to act. We need to connect like-minded champions and resource partners so each can bring what they can offer to the table. Each has to ask: What are my gifts? What do I see as the world's greatest need? How can I face my doubts to take the first step towards doing something about it today?

Perhaps that is what Singaporeans have to do today: to pause and reflect on the gifts we already have to offer. In fact, who we are is in itself a precious and priceless gift. Who can we bless with our skills, resources and with our presence? No one can do everything, but everyone can do something. It can be time, money or talent that we offer in service of one another. Let our goal be not only to be best in the world in our endeavours, but to be the best for the world and for each other. If we succeed, we will not need a "Singaporean of the Year" award to exemplify what it means to live the good life in Singapore.

Chapter 13

Returning to a Social Capital-Driven Vision of Fostering Inclusion in SGP 4.0*

Gerard Ee

*This article was originally published in Commentary, Volume 27 titled "SGP4.0: An Agenda" © 2018 The National University of Singapore Society. Gerard Ee heads Beyond Social Services, a charity dedicated to help children and youth from less privileged backgrounds break out of the poverty cycle.

In the 1980s when I was a youth worker, young people who did not have the benefit of succeeding in school got on in life by taking up a trade. If they were willing, it would not have been difficult by word of mouth to find plumbers, carpenters, electricians or other craftsmen to take them on as apprentices. Most of the youth who came to my programmes started off as painters and along the way picked up other skills that served them well in blue-collar work. Regardless of their personal or family challenges, they were optimistic that they would find a way to make a living and to build a life. These youth were more than aware of their low-income background, their lack of formal education, and their challenges with the English language, our *lingua franca*. However, they believed that with the support of family and friends, they would make progress. This was a belief rooted in the power of social capital.

Services Replace Natural Networks

Today, the structure of our economy and the demographics of our country are very different, and these realities exacerbate the disadvantages faced by our fellow citizens who lack formal education, those who are in the lower socio-economic strata let alone those with ill-health or disabilities. Caring for our fellow citizens on the margins is a perennial challenge, but the challenge I would like to highlight is the way we have been dealing with it in recent years.

According to the Ministry of Social and Family Development (MSF) website, there are currently more than 10,200 people employed in the social and community service sector and "it is a growing one with ample employment opportunities." The proliferation of services competes with natural support networks, replaces the notion of a caring community and its self-directed problem-solving, and does nothing to weave the social fabric that binds us as a cohesive society. Neither does it comfort those on the margins that they actually have a relationship or a bond with the mainstream as service consumption is often experienced as being problematised, fenced out, and contained in isolation.

The current social service ecosystem is designed on the basis of helping people cope with their environment. There is a focus on psychology and operates on the belief that problems require treatment or intervention provided by professionals or programmes. There is little focus on the context, circumstances or structural issues that sustain these problems. There is also no acknowledgement that Singapore's need for immigration to compensate for low birth rates and a shrinking workforce, on the other hand, contribute to a plural society that further stresses those on the margins and reinforces their sense of displacement within their own country.

Rally Society Around Social Issues

If social services are to serve as an important pillar for nation-building, then social inclusion and integration must be understood as efforts in creating an environment where no one feels displaced instead of simply trying to get the displaced to fit in. We must regard social issues not as problems to be fixed but as opportunities to rally society toward a common good as well as a shared future that is mutually satisfying and meaningful. It is an opportunity to weave and strengthen the social fabric among people from different backgrounds and reduce the threats and ill-effects that a plural society presents.

To achieve this, we must re-imagine the role of the social sector as one that increases the social capital within our country rather than one that simply services those on the margins. It will work at creating context and conditions that enable people from different segments and social strata to develop mutual trust and co-create solutions where they have an active role in their success.

When people come together to own and act on their shared concerns, they will experience a sense of connectedness and contentment which closes the social divide among them. For those on the margins, these relationships would be important in fostering social capital that avails them of opportunities and resources from outside their own circle of family and friends, to raise their sense of well-being.

Why should we do that? We live in an imperfect and unequal world but resentment and resignation set in when people, especially those on the margins, do not believe that their lives can change for the better. This happens when social services that are positioned to help those who have fallen behind communicate that their service-users have failed to fit in or to contribute to the larger scheme of things. This is reinforced when the process of accessing resources requires service-users to accentuate their needs. This makes the people involved feel like they or their situations are problems. They constantly surface "needs", which are the raw materials for the proliferation of service provision.

Combine Strengths to Build Value

A different paradigm in creating social services is to think of it as holding a space where a diverse group of people come together to make a difference to themselves and the group in a way they cannot when they act merely as individuals. It is inviting people to pool their strengths, gifts and talents in a manner that they find satisfying and meaningful.

In this vein, problem-solving efforts then become organised around the belief that all people, despite their challenges and often because of their challenges, have the potential to lead positive change. All of us have something of value to contribute and together we can build the community and country we want to belong to and live in.

In the public rental neighbourhoods my organisation works within, residents young and old are encouraged to gain an awareness of their shared concerns, deepen their understanding of the issues at hand, assume ownership of the situation and take action. With the support of volunteers and resources from the larger community, parents and youth come together to address issues such as poor school attendance, care and supervision of children, and substance use. As a result, parents coordinate learning and social programmes as well as organise themselves to support neighbours experiencing difficulties. People demonstrate leadership in surprisingly large measure, and neighbourhoods start to have a climate of kindness, generosity, cooperation and forgiveness. People have a sense that together with neighbours and others in the Singapore community, they are making life better for all.

Collective Effort for Change

Let me illustrate this paradigm with a tangible example: The Community Tabung is a savings programme that encourages low-income families to top-up their children's Child Development Account (CDA). Once a month on Tabung Counting Day, the children will pour their savings into a common pool in the presence of their parents and volunteers. The total amount is then divided equally among all who participated. Each child's amount is tripled by a donor and when deposited into their CDA, the initial shared savings would have multiplied six times at the end of the process as contributions to the individual child's account are then matched by the Government.

This programme has been designed to encourage personal and collective responsibility and while savings are important, there is also much value in the conversations people have about it and the relationships formed among all involved. Participants safeguard the practice of sharing the pooled savings equally as they appreciate the ebb and flow of life; its ups and downs. Thus, being a part of a community where there is much give and take is comforting and satisfying. On counting days, parents, donors and volunteers cooperate to get things going and the experience of organising a successful event is mutually rewarding. Also, as parents get to know each other, they begin looking out for each other's children.

Another initiative where success is a collective community effort would be our seasonal festive baking projects. To help low-income families earn some income, we secure orders of cookies from corporations as gifts during the festive periods. To handle the large orders, we cooperate with Caritas Singapore, the social and charitable arm of the Catholic Church to offer the use of their baking facility at Agape Village for free. Then, we welcome representatives from the Islamic Religious Council of Singapore to perform Sertu, a cleansing ritual which assures Muslims that the cookies prepared at their studio will be appropriate for their consumption. Also, as suppliers grant substantial discounts and volunteers offer labour and expertise, the low-income families have come to see that while hard work is necessary for success, it is not enough. There is also social capital or friendships where even religious differences and vested interests are put aside to facilitate their success.

In the current mainstream social service ecosystem, the goal is for those facing difficulties to behave differently and the significant relationship for them is the one they have with the professional assigned to assist them. Help is the domain of this expert and even if the difficulties are resolved, the approach does not build social capital that enhances their resilience or an improved perception of their circumstances. However, when the goal is for community and society to behave differently and when relationships between neighbours and fellow citizens have a significant impact on one's well-being, our social fabric is strengthened.

Network of Community Resources

Does this social capital-driven paradigm work? There is further evidence. In 2016, we embarked on a study to understand the value of our efforts in bridging low-income neighbourhoods with resources and relationships. After a year, there was a positive impact on residents' personal empowerment, their network of support and social connection, and their perception of their neighbourhood's characteristics. Respondents felt that where they lived, there was a sense of community, and mutual trust among neighbours.

Our work covers some 60 public rental housing blocks and our relationship with the relevant government and grassroots leaders is a hygiene factor for our continued presence. Where this relationship was not well established, our efforts made little headway. Otherwise, our work has been facilitated with the access to rooms, event halls and spaces for community engagement that those grassroots leaders help us with.

So, with these points in mind, let me make four recommendations to Singapore's fourth generation, or 4G leaders, to consider as they think about addressing the needs of those on the margins of society.

Retaining Community Spaces for Community Members

The first recommendation is for the 4G leaders to safeguard community resources and infrastructure for the efforts that bring those on the margins toward the centre of the community.

I find it disturbing to see community centres being leased out to fast food operators and other businesses. Surely, residents can go to the mall in the town centre should they desire such products and surely, the community centre management can utilise their facilities to reach out to residents who may find it difficult or not gratifying to visit the mall as a routine. In any case, community development and resident engagement can certainly be more than making it convenient for people to get fast food.

The optimising of community resources for rental revenue gives the impression that the Government is subsidising business at the expense of meaningful community engagement and development as it is not transparent how the revenue is ploughed back into the community apart from maintaining infrastructure. It also signals the depreciation of community as its space is being encroached upon or even colonised by commercial interest. If this is not the correct impression nor intent, the leaders should reassess some of their positions or decisions in these areas.

Harness Community Competence to Co-create Solutions

Next, our 4G leaders must safeguard the notion of community as one that has the competence to resolve its challenges; a place where people can give and receive support and build a satisfying and meaningful life as has been described above.

As such, the co-ordination of social services should put the power and decision-making of people at the front and centre of all efforts. Neighbours, families, friends and constituents, in spite of their own problems, can be equipped to act as front-line responders for those experiencing difficulties.

Leadership, in this light, is about convening gatherings where people from different socio-economic backgrounds and ethnicity can understand each other better and co-create solutions. The different gifts and relationships among constituents should be mapped, inventories should be set-up and updated regularly; these gifts and relationships should be celebrated, activated and treasured as assets a community can draw upon to solve its own problems or enrich its life.

Return Problems to the People

To activate a community's assets, the 4G leaders must also safeguard the transparency of concerns. What does this mean? Unless, concerns are clearly defined and acknowledged, people cannot or will not see the need to cooperate and resolve them. Usually when concerns are raised, our leaders cite a programme or scheme that is already dealing with it. This says that the status quo is good enough and no improvements are necessary.

I would suggest that the social service sector be an advocate that draws people's attention to the challenges facing citizens living on the margins. Then instead of recommending expert industry solutions, enable people to respond in a way where they can utilise their own competencies and social capital.

As such, this transparency of concerns would mean returning the problems to the people so that they can appreciate the implications and strengthen their sense of agency or ability to act on them. Leadership is about listening to aspirations and factors that people find motivating and then connecting them to relevant resources and relationships as a way of fuelling their work.

Winning Together

Lastly, our 4G leaders must safeguard a narrative of "finishing well together." Our leaders often use football and other sporting analogies to explain their roles and responsibilities. In sport, we must play to win and while winners are adored, so are the values of fair-play, sportsmanship, mutual respect, friendship and the solidarity among sportsmen, all of which define the context for excellence.

To draw on the philosophy of the Olympic movement, we must "create a way of life based on the joy found in effort, the educational value of good example and respect for universal fundamental ethical principles."[1] Our collective goal must be for everyone to reach the "finish line" of being recognised as a valuable citizen with much to contribute. The social service sector must stand together with those who have crossed the finish line to applaud those still running towards it as they make the effort to do the same.

Conclusion

I have presented four areas requiring guardianship and if they are indeed well safeguarded, the social service sector would have woven a social fabric that can be a safety net or trampoline for those on the margins. At the same time, there would be a heightened awareness and understanding of our social challenges across society. Also, people will not shy away from reclaiming these challenges as their own and as a result, start organising themselves to act on those challenges.

One visible indicator that we are succeeding will be the nature of the Annual Social Service Summit. Instead of it being attended only by social service professionals and leaders of social service organisations, it would feature those who have come together as a community to address their shared concerns. Leaders in the social service sector would be able to quantify how these efforts have contributed to nation-building and fortify the bedrock of compassion, social justice and community that social work is built upon.

---

[1] "Promote Olympism in Society," The International Olympic Committee, https://www.olympic.org/the-ioc/promote-olympism.

Chapter 14

Foundations: The Mutants of Democracy*

Lee Poh Wah

*This article was originally published in Commentary, Volume 25 titled "A Democracy of Deeds and Problem Solving" © 2016 The National University of Singapore Society. Lee Poh Wah is the Chief Executive Officer of the Lien Foundation.

The preschool at the void deck of Block 52, Lengkok Bahru looks like any other in Singapore. Pint-sized furniture fills its classrooms, and song and chatter echo off cheerily adorned walls.

Watch closely however, and things start to look a little out of place.

Some children are tucking into pretend meals while one child lifts two fingers to his lips and starts puffing on a pretend cigarette. Another plays with a doll, but in a strange, sexualised way. In art class, a boy draws a wonderful, soaring eagle, because he wants to fly home "when daddy beats mommy". Some children are formally enrolled, but attend classes only a handful of times a month or are habitually late, arriving hungry. When probed, the teachers reveal with stoicism and a hint of embarrassment, the verbal abuse they sometimes endure from parents.

In a neighbourhood where some of the nation's priciest condominiums are located, 40 percent of the children in this preschool come from families with monthly household incomes that are less than $1,000. Preschools such as these exist across Singapore, especially where Housing and Development Board (HDB) rental flats are located. Meritocratic Primary 1 has not even begun, and these children are already far behind.

Singapore needs to think differently about poverty I thought to myself after visiting that preschool in 2012. Poverty is not only about education and jobs — it is a disease; one that is invisible, infectious and often terminal. We have to find a vaccine, and I thought, the philanthropic foundation that I represent must find an answer.

Germ Theory Philanthropy

Philanthropic foundations can be good vehicles for tackling such ill-defined problems. After all, foundations' worldviews were historically shaped by germ theory. Conceived in the United States (US) at the turn of the 20th century, philanthropists such as Andrew Carnegie and John Rockefeller sought to do for society what scientists did for diseases: to go beyond symptoms, isolate the pathogen, and design a remedy.

They had reason for their fanfaronade. Foundations were the centres of plutocratic power that wielded outsized resources. They were opaque, free to intervene for the public good, with little accountability for what that meant exactly. Moreover, like some universities, they possessed the powers of immortality — they were structured legally and financially to last in perpetuity. Foundations were considered "mutants" and at conception, rejected by some as threats to democracy.

A century later, foundations have proliferated. In the United States alone, there were 86,000 foundations holding US$715 billion in assets as of 2012. The newest foundations are set up, not by white-haired tycoons, but by tech titans who speak of disruption, the same way they upended the world of business.

Yet, abundance and generosity have not been matched by clarity of purpose. Those running foundations tend to be tight-lipped about how they work and what they are attempting to accomplish. There is insufficient industry data and scrutiny by media and academia. In other words, this corner of the charity sector is shrouded in a mystery that rivals that of Wall Street. Little wonder that a century after their birth, foundations continue their struggle to attain legitimacy.

Yet, legitimacy is well within the mutants' reach. It rests ultimately on their ability to contribute to society in a way that is commensurate with their unique position. As Rob Reich, political science professor at Stanford University, pointed out in a 2013 Boston Review article, foundations should do more to leverage their freedom from the market and electoral accountability. As independent funders of diverse public goods, they provide alternative options to the solutions offered by the State, enlivening democracy and tempering government orthodoxy. Also, they possess the unfettered ability to engage in high-risk endeavours that impatient investors and fickle electorates shy away from.

In a "democracy of deeds" as espoused by one of our pioneer political leaders the late Mr S Rajaratnam, the bias towards action plays squarely to the strengths of foundations. At the Lien Foundation (hereinafter referred to as "Foundation"), we have tried to step up to this challenge.

Established in 1980, the Foundation has narrowed its focus over the years. Today, we work in just three areas — early childhood education, eldercare, and water and sanitation — and within each area, on neuralgic and niche issues. We typically conceptualise our own projects with partners that we choose to work with. This essay shares some of our work in early childhood education and hopefully provides both a sense of our philosophical approach and our experience with project implementation.

Apartheid in Singapore

At Lengkok Bahru, we spent months hunkered down with the preschool team to understand the true nature of the problem. For these children, disruptive behavior was a manifestation of instability at home, caused by factors such as single parenthood, family violence, incarceration, substance addiction, unemployment and mental health problems. These conditions were breeding what Harvard professor Robert Putnam termed "incipient class apartheid" right here in Singapore.

In our view, the preschool is the best place for intervention because it is a naturalistic and controlled setting where children spend hours daily. To be effective, however, it would require deploying specialists from other disciplines into the preschool to support the over-worked and demoralised teachers. It was a model that Care Corner, the nonprofit organisation that ran the preschool, believed in, but was unable to execute because of government funding guidelines.

A grant from the Foundation provided the latitude to try something different. Named "Circle Of Care" (COC), the new programme adopted an ecological approach, bringing educational therapists, social workers and preschool teachers, who typically work apart, together as a unique multi-disciplinary team around the child at the preschool. The teacher-child ratio was lowered, the level of parental engagement was raised and community resources such as artists, librarians and volunteers, were mobilised.

Not everything went smoothly. High staff turnover caused by the toxic school environment resulted in starts and stops in the work. Among the professionals in the newly-assembled multi-disciplinary team, childhood poverty became the proverbial elephant to the blind, as each interpreted its cause and remedy through different lens. Above all, it emerged, as we began work, that the needs faced by the children and families were more severe than what appeared on the surface.

Two years of perseverance brought encouraging results.

Participation in parent-teacher conferences (PTCs) crept up from a shocking zero to more than 50 percent as teachers waylaid parents on their way home for impromptu PTCs in the void decks. As social workers, who now represented the preschool, knocked on door after door to introduce themselves, school attendance for chronic absentees rose from 30 percent to 70 percent, even as their families continued battling challenges relating to health, finances, employment and housing.

Educational therapists introduced fresh techniques — such as talking puppets — into the school to kindle a love of learning among children from poor homes devoid of books.

To our surprise and relief, children who were mere months from the start of Primary One made leaps in numeracy and literacy skills. At night, they would show off their newly found reading, writing and counting skills at home, to the delight of their parents.

Multiplying Mutation

In 2015, halfway through the programme, we decided to scale it up. Our target: at least 15 new COC preschools within three years. Care Corner boldly relinquished its preschool operations to focus on turning COC from a project into a service offered to other preschool operators. The knowledge, so painstakingly acquired on the ground, was institutionalised in a training programme to introduce this emerging approach to social workers, teachers and therapists. A longitudinal study was commissioned to track the children we have worked with till they are in Primary Three.

A key plank in the strategy is to involve primary schools in preserving the hard won progress made by these children in their preschool years under COC. To do so requires skirting round the current lack of a formal system of information-sharing and collaboration between the preschool sector and primary schools.

Presently, at Primary One registration, many at-risk children can be identified through the required paperwork, but many others whose circumstances are not easily gleaned from formal documents fall through the cracks. These children miss out on services they need, such as pastoral care and counseling, even though they are available. Only later, at the end of Primary One or in Primary Two, are they identified through the emergence of chronic problems such as absenteeism and misbehaviour. Precious time and opportunities will have been wasted, and the primary schools spend the next few years on the back foot, helping such children level up.

Our solution rests on the hypothesis that where we find a primary school with a higher-than-average proportion of at-risk children, we will also find preschools with similar populations. In such locations, we plan to build a cluster of COC preschools that would feed an anchor COC primary school, via a structured, formalised system of information-sharing and joint care of the child between the primary school welfare personnel and COC social workers. Working with the Ministry of Education machinery took patience, but two primary schools came on board.

Complicating the Narrative

Schools and the education system more broadly, are an important part of the solution, but cannot be depended on as the great equaliser in society. Our hope is that in time, COC will not only close a gap in our education system, but also change society's views towards poverty. Today's dominant narrative suggests that kids with tough childhoods do badly because of bad role models and bad choices. Studies reveal a more complex dynamic at play.

In the 1990s, the landmark Adverse Childhood Experiences (ACE) Study completed by Centers for Disease Control and Prevention and Kaiser Permanente's Health Appraisal Clinic in San Diego had already managed to quantify the long-term effect of abuse and neglect on children. Those who experienced at least four ACEs or forms of childhood trauma, out of a maximum of 10, were already twice as likely to be smokers, 12 times more likely to have attempted suicide, seven times more likely to be alcoholic, and 10 times more likely to be drug abusers.

Another startling study by University of Wisconsin-Madison neuroscientist Seth Pollak found that children from poor families have smaller brains. Through magnetic resonance imaging scans, Dr Pollak discovered that the regional grey matter volumes in the brains of children below the US federal poverty level were eight to 10 percent below the developmental norm.

Yet another study by Victor Carrion, Director of the Stanford Early Life Stress and Pediatric Anxiety Programme, found that chronic or unresolved trauma changes a child's levels of cortisol, the stress hormone, wrecking havoc on the developing hippocampus, pre-frontal cortex and amygdala, the parts of the brain that control memory, decision-making, and fear. Children with childhood trauma struggle with learning, managing gratification and taming impulsivity in their adulthood. Some are even misdiagnosed with special needs as a result.

Apart to a Part

Besides disabilities caused by poverty, the Foundation has an advocacy programme on disabilities caused by genetics. We noticed in Singapore that there is another silent sandwiched class that is squeezed not between income levels, but between abilities. Children with severe special needs are on the radar of the Government. However, children with mild special needs stay under the radar. Their conditions, although manageable or treatable, often go unidentified and deteriorate due to a lack of awareness and access to screening.

This was the reason why in 2009, the Foundation partnered with the KK Women's and Children's Hospital and the PAP Community Foundation on the "Mission: I'mPossible" (MIP) programme to provide screening and intervention for children with mild special needs. A simple factor differentiated it from existing services: Location.

Like COC, the screening and intervention of MIP was based within the naturalistic setting of preschools, instead of hospitals or clinics. A team comprising a paediatrician, a psychologist, a speech and language therapist, an occupational therapist and a learning support facilitator would provide therapy and train teachers. Senior teachers were appointed as Learning Support Educators and tasked with integrating therapy goals into classroom routines.

It also proved to be a cost-effective model. Kicking off with 25 preschools, the programme was eventually adopted by the Government, renamed the "Development Support Programme", and scaled up to 400 preschools in 2015. An additional 600 preschools are in the pipeline.

As a signatory to the United Nations' Convention on the Rights of Persons with Disabilities that commits our country to ensuring that such people enjoy full equality under the law, Singapore can do even better. Unlike the children in MIP, many children with moderate to severe special needs struggle to even find a preschool willing to accept them.

A handful of exclusive preschools do offer a high-quality inclusive experience, but at a hefty price. This is the reason why some parents opt for home-schooling. Others simply but erroneously treat intervention sessions as a form of preschool education. Like the children in COC, theirs is a ghettoised childhood, spent apart from peers.

To address the needs of this other segment, the Foundation partnered AWWA (formerly known as Asian Women's Welfare

Association) and government agency, SG Enable, in 2014 to develop Kindle Garden, a preschool with an inclusive educational model. The school caters to 75 children; 70 percent of them will be typically-developing children and 30 percent will have special needs. It features open-concept classrooms, an outdoor treehouse accessible by wheelchair, and therapy equipment disguised as play-forms to eliminate both the physical need for therapy rooms and the invisible stigma they create among adults and children.

Kindle Garden operates with a higher teacher-student ratio than the norm and counts specialists and health professionals on its staff. A specially designed curriculum enables learning across abilities. The hope is that it will be a place where special needs children can develop functional skills, independence and friendships while typically-developing children learn the values of respect, generosity and responsibility.

Kindle Garden was an instant draw for parents of special needs children: over 100 queued for a place after announcement of its launch. Marketing efforts were therefore directed at parents of typically-developing children, highlighting the 1,100 sq m space, double the size of a typical preschool in a HDB void deck that was designed by President's Design Award-winning architects. Its fees are pegged just slightly above the median industry fee of $900.

To our surprise, the parents streamed in. As of February 2016, a month after opening, 55 of the 75 spaces have been taken. To keep to our planned ratio of typically-developing and special needs children, we will be able to take in more special needs children as typically-developing children enrol.

Internally, the team continues to grapple with tough questions, both philosophical and operational. With special needs differing by category and severity, what would be an optimal mix for each class to be fair and effective to all? Is selecting children from the waitlist based on our idea of an optimal class mix instead of their queue position inherently uninclusive? Are our teachers truly ready to effectively manage a class comprising, say, one child with Down's

Syndrome and another with Autism, alongside other naturally boisterous children?

Whatever answers we arrive at, there are ultimately only so many inclusive preschools that Singapore can build. The sustainable solution will be a combination of more inclusive schools and an expanded Development Support Programme that offers on-site intervention for children with not only mild, but also moderate, special needs.

Advocate Adequately

In COC, MIP and Kindle Garden, the common thread is early intervention. Addressing achievement gaps early reaps dividends many times over in later years for individuals, families and the economy. That is because children from low-income families and special needs children are almost always haunted by life's early setbacks, long after their fleeting childhoods. Marriages break up; caregivers burn out. Support from donors and well-wishers wanes as toddlers become awkward teenagers and burly adults. Addiction to video games is emerging as a problem for such children as it provides the illusion of an alternative universe where they can finally find mastery over their bodies and destinies.

Many such stories are untold, and many more exist.

That is why at the Foundation, we view advocacy as a cornerstone of philanthropy. Done effectively, it brings the weight of public opinion to bear on the challenge at hand, dispelling tendencies of complacency and mediocrity, and keeping the Government's hot seat, hot.

An example of such advocacy was the Starting Well Index, the first global ranking of early childhood education that we commissioned the Economist Intelligence Unit to conduct. Out of 45 countries analysed, Singapore came in a dismal 29th place, behind the Special Administrative Region of Hong Kong and debt-ridden Greece.

In a ranking-obsessed society such as ours, the distillation of a complex problem into a single number brought sudden clarity. How could a country with an airport, schools and quality of life ranked among the world's best, accept sub-par preschools? The thought itself was heart-rending.

After the release of the Index, we followed up quickly with two supporting reports: "Vital Voices" which featured the improvements suggested by 27 leaders from Singapore's preschool sector, and a survey of parents that revealed a majority preference for greater government involvement in preschool education. The trio (the Index and the two reports) offered the impartiality of statistics and the diversity of views from a democratic collection of voices.

Some months later, a number of new government initiatives were announced to uplift the preschool sector. Many observers credited this to the Foundation, but to do so would be simplistic. To be fair, the Government had studied the issue at length prior to the arrival of the Index, but perhaps the Index brought useful clarity, urgency and greased the wheels of change.

Radically Practical

At the Foundation, we favour contribution over attribution.

Philanthropy should, after all, be about liberating the receiver, and never about redeeming the giver. To liberate, we need to give courage to the people on the front line of social change who know the ground realities best, by assuring them that it is safe to fail with us. We encourage them to take risks and think the unthinkable. Our relationship is not coloured by a belief in the simplicity of cause and effect, but by the warmth and banter of an intuitive grant-making approach that is anchored in trust, transparency and chemistry. Internally, we are proponents of social pedagogy, the discipline that draws on core theories from education, sociology, psychology, philosophy and others in tackling social problems. In this worldview, humanistic principles are not a luxury, but essential. It is the harder path to take, and the Foundation has had as many home runs as spectacular failures. We share our lessons freely, not as a choice, but as a duty for the status we occupy as a foundation in Singapore. Even mutants must mutate and unlearning is just as important as learning.

In the final analysis, no matter how hard we try, silver bullets do not exist.

Just as we were all geared up to scale the COC, we received sobering news. A child whose parent was in jail, but who was nonetheless holding up well and turning out to be one of the brightest in class, was discovered to have been molested by a neighbour. Once the poster child of the COC programme, she now undergoes counselling at the Institute of Mental Health.

Chapter 15

Locating the Heart of Civic Action: A Tale from Cassia Crescent*

Lim Jingzhou and Rocky Howe

*This article was originally published in Commentary, Volume 27 titled "SGP4.0: An Agenda" © 2018 The National University of Singapore Society. Lim Jingzhou, an active volunteer since 2013, co-founded the Cassia Resettlement Team. Having a diverse range of interests, Rocky Howe engaged in research on the Cassia Resettlement Team and pursued studies in Politics, Philosophy, and Law at King's College London at the time of writing.

The Cassia Resettlement Team (CRT) serves residents of Blk 52 Cassia Crescent, a majority of whom have been relocated from the rental housing estates of Dakota Crescent and Sims Drive.

Through weekly house visits to our residents, and other initiatives such as potluck parties with the community, we learn about and address the needs and challenges they face. We also seek to work collaboratively with various community partners, including formal social service organisations and government stakeholders, as we do so. Ultimately, CRT's objectives are to walk the journey of life with the residents and facilitate the growth of communities.

We write this account as individual members of CRT reflecting on our collective work, in the hope of speaking with rather than for the team. Our views do not reflect the full diversity of perspectives at CRT, nor the fact that its members have different motivations to serve, participate in, and bring about social change.

We begin with this acknowledgement of difference because it is crucial to what we do. Having engaged more than a 100 volunteers of various backgrounds including students, working professionals from different sectors, and even the residents of Blk 52 themselves, we are glad that our brand of ground-up civic action is achieving an integrative and transformative role — bringing together the perspectives, experiences and skills of various members who might not ordinarily have had the opportunity to interact with and learn from one another.

Hence this account is but one interpretation of the CRT story. We would like it to provide a picture of the possibilities for better and greater civic action around people, places and communities in the Singapore of the future.

Finding Roots — Resettlement, Change and Identity

Many of our early members found their way to CRT through the efforts of various ground-up initiatives that emerged in the rental housing estate of Dakota Crescent after its redevelopment was announced by the Housing and Development Board (HDB) in

2014. Its residents were asked to relocate to new rental flats nearby in Cassia Crescent, or rental flats in other HDB estates elsewhere.

Those civic initiatives included *IgnorLAND of its Loss*, a community-engaged arts project by theatre company, Drama Box that culminated in a site-specific theatre performance connecting the public with the place and people of Dakota Crescent.[1]

Similarly, *Dakota Adventures* created tours of Dakota Crescent co-guided by the residents themselves, giving them a platform to share their personal stories with tour participants.[2] *Between Two Homes* was a documentary effort where residents were invited to share their stories and relocation experiences for an interactive website.[3]

These efforts resulted in the formation of a wide network of volunteers and participants, some of whom gradually coalesced to form CRT. These shifted the narrative about Dakota Crescent from being just about heritage conservation to a concern with the lives of the members of the Dakota Crescent community and the challenges they faced before, during and after relocation. It is the residents' needs, above all else, that are at the core of CRT's focus.

It is not that heritage conservation advocacy is unimportant. Rather, we think the shift towards a concern for people is a natural turn that reflects the inclinations of a younger generation of Singaporeans who have at most, a passing connection to the physical place. For them, Dakota Crescent links them to contemporary social and political issues like ageing and loneliness, and offers a richer space for civic action to emerge.

Building Communities of Care

It was only after the residents of Dakota Crescent relocated into Blk 52 that CRT was formally organised and when we began to realise

[1] "IgnorLAND of its Loss," Drama Box, http://www.dramabox.org/eng/productions-ignorland-loss.html.

[2] "Dakota Adventures," In Facebook [Dakota Adventures], https://www.facebook.com/pg/dakotadventures/about/?ref=page_internal.

[3] Run & Gun Media and Dakota Adventures, "Between Two Homes," http://betweentwohomes.sg/.

the complexity of the challenges they faced. They had difficulty adapting to a radically different environment which was even more acutely felt as the relocation had disrupted their sources of formal and informal social support.

We were clear from the outset that CRT would not replace the role of traditional social service organisations, but instead, that we would act as intermediaries to help these formal agencies bridge the gaps that emerged in supporting the residents. Yet we found ourselves, in many instances, also taking up direct responsibility of care for particularly vulnerable residents of Blk 52 given the various limitations of the current social welfare system. These were instances when our volunteers rallied together to discuss the best course of action to address the needs that emerged.

When we did that, we often found ourselves trying to balance between addressing a particular need that emerged directly and creating unhealthy dependence on volunteers by the residents. We were also keen to avoid taking over the type of duties and responsibilities that ought to have been provided by social service or public agencies, such as medical escorts to hospitals for the residents. We would make an effort to highlight residents' needs to such agencies so that they could take the appropriate action, unless it was particularly urgent.

Our volunteers have also gotten together out of their own initiative to develop new projects for the community. One such programme is *LIVE@52*, consisting of small-scale activities that target residents from a few floors or of a specific demographic profile, such as children. These activities, largely art-based and held at different spaces within the community, aim to reach out to residents and deepen relationships across the block.

Twinkle Wishes is another example. This project team provides end-of-life support to residents, increasing awareness and access to planning instruments such as Advanced Care Planning and the Lasting Power of Attorney. This arose from the recognition that many residents who had end-of-life wishes did not know how to use these instruments to ensure that their wishes would eventually be honoured.

We are heartened to see that a strong sense of community has emerged among our volunteers as they worked together in the ways we have mentioned above. The collective action around Blk 52 has been transformative for each one of us, opening up conversations about a range of different challenges people face — from housing to ageing to healthcare. It has led us to build collective knowledge around social issues that question and challenge existing narratives and policy approaches. It has helped us develop a sense of agency that tells us we can believe in our ability to care for others and advocate social change.

At the heart of our work is the time volunteers spend with residents during our visits and through our programmes. Such interactions are not merely instrumental. Our volunteers build genuine relationships with residents at Blk 52 which create a deeper understanding of who they are as individuals, rather than as clients or passive recipients of care. Through our interactions, we also learn from their life stories.

What has emerged in CRT is a community of care that places each resident and the wider community of Blk 52 at the centre of it. We think that the future of civic action is tied to building such communities of care. Care becomes a space of action and an opportunity for change. We imagine that such communities, when driven by action and processes of genuine interaction with others, are well-suited to creating social inclusion and solidarity in practice.

The Conditions for Transformative Civic Action

In the course of our work at Blk 52, we have encountered many members of the public and government agencies who are supportive of our work. We have had individuals share valuable ideas, wisdom and the resources that we needed. For instance, there have been civil servants who have acted as navigators when we negotiated with various departments and agencies about different matters on behalf of the residents.

Such successes have often been contingent on a range of factors — personal relationships with individuals in different organisations; the goodwill of particular civil servants we came into contact with; and sometimes what seemed like sheer luck. This is because ground-up initiatives, lacking legal recognition, tend not to have the same degree of legitimacy in the eyes of public agencies. On first contact, there is often scepticism about our intentions and an aversion to sharing information that we think would facilitate better coordination in meeting the needs of residents.

This, in our view, is not sustainable for civic action in the long run as it creates both a high barrier to entry for civic actors, and a lack of certainty and predictability in engagement with the state. We recognise that it does take time to build trust between existing public agencies and the social sector when the civic actor is new. We would like to suggest that the network needs a wider definition of legitimacy than a formal organisation does — that definition could take into account the record of the civic actors on the ground as well as the preferences of the community itself.

Making civic action sustainable also involves seeing such actors as equal partners in shaping the social space. Equality can be fostered by allowing for an open and transparent exchange of information between the state and civic actors. It should also come from recognising how the latter can be a valuable source of community knowledge and therefore a legitimate contributor to policy discussions; they are not just hands and legs on the ground.

The next, fourth generation of political leaders can pave the way for the rise of civic actors by lowering the barriers to entry and fostering an open and collaborative approach to addressing social issues. Yet such change also requires a more fundamental shift in the political narrative — leaders must move away from simplistic narratives of progress and success, to allow for better acknowledgement and recognition of the unmet needs of Singaporeans and the difficulty our society faces in resolving them. Only with such honest and transparent engagement will civic actors feel confident enough to engage the state.

We make these suggestions to encourage the formation of civic groups and improve their effectiveness in bringing about social change. But it is also important to look beyond the policy and social goals such actors might have in order to recognise the intrinsic value of civic action in building community and forging a sense of belonging.

In an era where we see rising political and social divisions across the world, civic action points the way to a rebuilding of social solidarity and inclusion through action and change. Civic action that has at its heart, the building of communities of care, as we have highlighted, offers citizens the full richness of being members of a social network and helps them uncover the value of individuals' experiences, needs, and diversity. We hope that CRT's work is at least a small contribution to imagining this better future.

Chapter 16

Transient Workers Count Too's Singaporean Way with Advocacy on Migrant Workers*

John Gee

---

* This article was originally published in Commentary, Volume 25 titled "A Democracy of Deeds and Problem Solving" © 2016 The National University of Singapore Society. John Gee has lived in Singapore since 1999 and has been an active member of Transient Workers Count Too since it was founded. He was President of the society from 2007 to 2011 and currently heads its Research Sub-committee.

Change Through Words and Deeds

Transient Workers Count Too (TWC2) was formed by people who felt stirred to action by stories of the mistreatment of migrant workers they had heard of or read about, as well as by personally witnessing what one of our early members called "the silent indignities" that these workers all too often faced. The group might have concentrated solely on providing material help to workers in distressing conditions, but, right from the outset, members thought that something more was needed.

We were determined to work for the elimination or alleviation, at its roots, of the host of problems that we saw. Advocacy, directed at changing policies and practices governing the status of migrant workers, was to be at the heart of our work. The logic is plain: it is similar to the distinction that can be made in the sphere of aid programmes between feeding hungry people and helping them to develop the capability to feed themselves. Advocacy focused on policies and practices can consume time and energy without producing visible results quickly, but it has the long-term potential to benefit far more individuals than emergency assistance programmes directed at addressing just the immediate needs of the migrant workers we wished to serve.

This did not mean ignoring the need to provide such direct assistance of course. Indeed, what we called "direct services" soon took up the lion's share of our resources and continues to do so. It did mean however ensuring that we kept advocacy firmly in view, and not allowing the pressures (and sometimes, satisfaction) of providing direct assistance to cause us to lose sight of the need for advocacy.

We defined TWC2's role as promoting the rights and well-being of migrant workers through advocacy (including public education), research and direct services. Rather than being three separate parallel areas of activity, we saw them as intertwined and mutually supportive. Our direct services work showed us the real problems that workers faced, including workers' own attitudes towards their kind. That, in turn, informed our research work and both the direct services and research underpinned our advocacy work.

Dealing with History — Dialogue and Trust-Building

TWC2 began in 2003 as The Working Committee Two, taking its name from an earlier civil society initiative. It was essentially planned as a nine-month campaign to promote better conditions and treatment for domestic workers. The group organised meetings and outreach efforts to the public, as well as actively engaged the media. We knew then we needed to communicate with the Government, but wondered if the Government would communicate with TWC2 in return?

It must be remembered that the "Marxist Conspiracy" of 1987 had a dampening effect on civil society in Singapore especially with regard to advocacy related to migrant workers. At the turn of the millennium, supporters of various causes were still exploring the space for activism; cautiously testing its boundaries. Even in 2003, there were those who were worried that an open initiative that questioned policies towards foreign domestic workers, might encounter a strongly hostile official response, or maybe, simply be ignored.

In the event, we approached the Ministry of Manpower (MOM), the chief government body that deals with migrant workers. This resulted in a meeting between TWC2 representatives and senior personnel of MOM in June 2003, followed by a fuller meeting in November the same year.

Those early meetings were valuable in starting a dialogue. There was wariness on both sides initially, but face-to-face conversations largely helped us overcome that. These meetings set something of a pattern for dialogue in the years that followed.

When we wished to meet, we would set out what we wanted to discuss clearly in advance. This was to everyone's advantage since MOM's spokespeople would be able to give us more considered and informative responses, having had the opportunity to consult colleagues before the meeting and ensure that they were thoroughly informed of government thinking at the time.

One important element in our approach to advocacy has been our positivity. It was evident to us from early on that the MOM and other government agencies were particularly sensitive to criticism that appeared purely negative, and that appeared as accusations.

Criticism was better received when it was, as MOM officials expressed it, "constructive", or, as we saw it, associated with proposals for positive and realistic alternatives.

From our point of view, bringing forward such proposals was fine: it was just what we wanted to do. It has required a lot of work by us over the years. Some ideas for reform seem common sense, but normally, there are arguments for the status quo that have weight and which need a response. A proposal for a change in law or regulations has to be firstly underpinned by evidence that there is a problem that needs attention, and then, by a reasoned and factually-based argument that the alternative we propose is an improvement that is not only desirable, but workable.

Besides making proposals for individual reforms (such as for safe and decent transportation for workers or itemised pay slips for all low-paid workers), we have prepared carefully reasoned proposals for the amendment of the major pieces of Singapore's legislation affecting migrant workers, including the Employment of Foreign Manpower Act, Employment Act and Employment Agencies Act using the same approach.

This has been a rather Singaporean approach to working for change. Internationally, many non-governmental organisations (NGOs) argue for reform on the basis of principles represented in human rights treaties and declarations, but this can seem abstract to many people and unpersuasive. Whether dealing with the Government or public in Singapore, we have found that laying stress on practical proposals for change was much more fruitful. More people listened instead of switching off. It was not that we ignored human rights standards. We have instead referred to them and called for them to be observed. By giving practical form to individual human rights standards, we have made more progress than if we had simply reiterated demands for Singapore to sign this convention or that treaty.

Our most protracted campaign has been over the question of a weekly day off for domestic workers. The rights argument was clear to everyone from the outset — the MOM's position (not strongly expressed to the public) was that, in principle, it was in favour of domestic workers having regular days off, but that there were significant practical obstacles in the way. In particular, it cited the needs of families that had children and elderly or disabled members who needed constant attention.

We argued that this did not seem to account for over half of all domestic workers, not having any days off and that, in any case, these workers who were called upon to provide constant care for family members were precisely the ones most in need of a break. In the recent past, we have come forward with ideas, including expanded social care, a more flexible system of domestic worker or care worker employment, as well as an adjustment of family arrangements and responsibilities to address the roadblocks facing the other half of domestic workers who seem to be so indispensable that a weekly day off would be regarded as an impossibility by their employers. If these other structures and programmes could be put in place, they could help employers overcome the final practical objections to all domestic workers having a weekly day off.

One problem for NGOs in dealing with a government body in any country is how to balance the public and private campaigning discussion which is definitely a problem in the Singapore context. Perhaps from the Government's point of view, closed-door dialogues allow an exchange of views in which officials can take a more nuanced and less rigid stand on policy and regulation than they usually would in a public forum. They might also take such dialogues as venues for testing the waters: unveiling official thinking on a change or initiative that is still being discussed or refined. They do not want anything such as the latter to be brought to media and public attention before or unless they feel absolutely ready.

NGOs that engage in advocacy, by contrast, tend to have more of a culture of openness. They are usually quite comfortable with being challenged and responding publicly to what they believe and do. They would prefer to be able to air exchanges with the Government on policies, regulations and their practical implementation fairly and freely. However, they have to face the challenge that dialogue with the Government usually involves a certain level of non-disclosure to the public as a pre-requisite.

It is probably futile to seek a complete meeting of minds on this question, so the two parties will simply have to bump along and improvise, meeting by meeting, letter by letter. In practice, it is usually not a big problem. TWC2 has found that normally, the broader questions that it would wish to broach in a public context, including on its website, can be raised with reference to statements and documents that are already in the public domain, but anything that is strictly "behind closed doors" material has to remain that way. There have been frustrations on both sides. The MOM officials become irritated from time to time when articles are published on our website criticising its handling of a worker's case and they feel that either the criticism is unwarranted, or that TWC2 ought to have raised the matter directly with the Ministry and not aired it in public. From TWC2's point of view, such articles can highlight particular issues in order to raise public awareness of them whilst promoting long-term change. In any case, the question remains of how far a dynamic, "newsy" website that supports the society's advocacy efforts should curtail the reports of a variety of writers with the stories real workers have told them — this is provided that due effort has been made to fact-check the circumstances related to the news item.

On the other hand, TWC2 has sometimes raised questions and received a non-response, a pretty uninformative statement that leaves us no wiser than before. Some of the questions raised on the website that have been a cause of irritation have, in fact, been raised in more general terms previously, without any significant progress being made towards resolving them.

What is important here is that there needs to be acceptance on both sides — relations between the Government and NGOs that engage in advocacy are bound to be a bit rocky — but we can live with that. If there is the will to engage and strive to make progress, these differences will not stop that.

Activities that can positively influence public opinion have been important in TWC2's work. From the outset, we tried our best to be helpful to students, researchers and journalists who sought information. We have often provided speakers to schools, colleges and other institutions. We regularly issue media releases and write to the press. Our research is partially geared to putting sound information into the public domain and promoting a better understanding of migrant workers.

The interaction of a steady stream of citizens with migrant workers is a by-product of some of our programmes. These include: The Cuff Road Project, that provides food daily to destitute workers; Discover Singapore, which provides a day out to somewhere interesting for destitute workers awaiting settlement of their cases; and others where many volunteers engage with migrant workers for the first time in their lives, giving them a new personal outlook towards migrant workers in general. They take their experiences away with them into whatever walk of life they are in, wherever they are, influencing others as they go.

Overall, such initiatives have value in themselves and they also contribute towards our advocacy goals — after all, a government considering possible changes in policy towards migrant workers has to take public opinion into account. Hence, if the public becomes more sympathetic towards these workers or concerned at particular violations of their rights, it can only work in favour of regulatory changes that we would regard as positive.

For new activists, advocacy work can seem quite frustrating, precisely because it rarely yields quick and visible results. When gains are made, they tend to be little by little and rarely result in an NGO winning 100 percent of what it set out to achieve. That has certainly been the case in Singapore: when we see progress, it is generally a small move here or an adjustment there that do not seem at all radical, but their cumulative impact can be considerable. Activists also have to reconcile themselves to the fact that government bodies in any country are not normally forthcoming about what did bring about a desired change — though it might be something that an NGO has devoted a lot of effort to achieving, it can feel, to the NGO's supporters, that their efforts are unrecognised. While this can be frustrating, it is the bigger picture that counts: the change did happen!

Sustaining TWC2's Success

So, with that caveat, it is possible to look back on TWC2's years of advocacy, research and public education tied to our direct services, and see that there have been successes however incomplete some have been: a mandatory day off policy that has significantly increased the percentage of domestic workers having a rest day; raised standards of protection against accidents and the elements for workers travelling to and from worksites; raised safety standards for domestic workers employed in high-rise buildings; faster resolution of cases for workers with complaints against their employers; stiffer penalties in the Employment Act against the demands of kickbacks from workers; the impending introduction of itemised payslips for workers on low salaries; and an anti-trafficking act. These and more were goals for which TWC2 worked, and on which our views were presented to MOM and other governmental institutions.

In our earlier years, we used to meet NGO activists from other countries and hear about their activities. Some organised demonstrations and rallies, and they issued strong public declarations demanding action from their governments. We would explain that we were working in an environment where this was either not possible or was likely to be counter-productive. Then we would tell them how we operated. TWC2's efforts often seemed very tame alongside theirs — we wrote a letter; we published an article; we issued a report or we had a closed-door meeting. Yet, it has turned out that we could have an impact and the work that we have done has gained respect.

At the same time, we must admit that our long-haul approach has not been without its difficulties. Early on, when our direct services work had only just started but when we were already engaging in advocacy, there were some who thought that TWC2 was "all talk". Volunteers have tended to be drawn towards work that they see as a direct assistance to workers in need. Their contributions have been of immense value and allowed us to do far more than would otherwise have been possible with our slender resources of paid staff and money.

However, we also need to maintain an organisation and sustain the other aspects of our work. We have had difficulties in building a core group of members to sustain our information services and advocacy. The main difference, in this respect, between our position in our earlier years and now, is that we can look back on a record of achievement that demonstrates that our overall approach has worked. That ought to be persuasive enough in helping us to renew and revitalise the organisation in years to come — though not for too many years, as our ultimate goal is to be so successful that our work will no longer be necessary!